Praise for Kerry Dalzotto and *Seeds for Tomorrow*

"I have known Kerry for many years and have admired the depth of her ability to convey a message from the heart. She is an excellent teacher and is passionate about the work that she does and wanting to bring it into the world. Her message is especially valuable for women at this time in history."

—Denise Linn, Author

SEEDS for TOMORROW

HOW TO ACCESS YOUR POWER AND POTENTIAL TO CREATE LASTING HAPPINESS

KERRY DALZOTTO

Copyright © 2023 by Kerry Dalzotto
Publisher: Star Topaz Publishing
Cover design: Openbook Howden Print & Design
Interior design: Openbook Howden Print & Design
Author Image: Bohemian Ekko Creative

All rights reserved. No part of this book may be reproduced by any mechanical, photographic, or electronic process, or in the form of a phonographic recording; nor may it be stored in a retrieval system, transmitted, or otherwise be copied for public or private use – other than for "fair use" as brief quotations embodied in articles and reviews – without prior written permission.

The author of this book does not dispense medical advice or prescribe the use of any technique as a form of treatment for any physical or emotional or medical condition without the advice of a health care professional, either directly or indirectly. Please also consult your health care professional prior to using essential oils while pregnant or breast feeding.

The intent of the author is only to offer information of a general nature to help you in your quest for emotional, physical, and spiritual well-being. In the event you use any of the information in this book for yourself, the author assumes no responsibility for your actions.

 A catalogue record for this book is available from the National Library of Australia

ISBN: 978-0-6458727-0-5
E-Book ISBN: 978-0-6458727-1-2

Designed and printed by:

 openbook howden print & design | 2-14 Paul Street St Marys SA 5042
T 08 8124 0000 F 08 8277 2354
openbookhowden.com.au

*This book is dedicated to my husband, Gianni
and my daughter, Cara.
Their constant love and support enriches my soul.*

CONTENTS

Introduction: The Goddess Journey Awakens 9

Chapter 1: Wounds of the Womb 13

Chapter 2: Cycling Towards Empowerment 43

Chapter 3: By the Light of the Moon 61

Chapter 4: The Gift of Menopause 77

Chapter 5: The Way of the Ancients 97

Chapter 6: Remembering Who You Are 107

Chapter 7: Awakening the Inner Goddess 129

Chapter 8: Journey of the Triple Goddess 155

Chapter 9: The Path of Forgiveness 175

Chapter 10: The Spirit Guide Connection 191

Chapter 11: Healing with Nature 215

Chapter 12: The Sisterhood Movement 233

Chapter 13: Living the Way of the Goddess 251

Afterword 269

Acknowledgements 275

Resources 277

INTRODUCTION

The Goddess Journey Awakens

Women are hard wired for connection. We crave it and have done it since the beginning of time. We crave deep soul connection to ourselves and heart-to-heart connection to other women within our close communities and those far and wide. Throughout our time during the COVID-19 pandemic, it highlighted the human need we have for connection to ourselves and to others to thrive in this world of ours.

We are at a pivotal time on our planet where the divine feminine is rising. Women are now standing up for what they believe in and finding the essence of who they are at their core. There has never been a more significant time on Mother Earth to dive deep within the waters of the feminine psyche to express to the world in our own unique and beautiful way who we are, what we desire, and our undeniable need to encapsulate our womanly worth.

Creativity is our birthright. Each of us is a creative being, and as women, the seat of our creativity lies within our womb space. Here in this sacred and hallowed place, we may birth the seeds of creation, whether those seeds are bringing children into the world or birthing a business, a relationship, or an idea for the future. Whatever your creative endeavour is, it all begins within the womb, the fertile soil of the soul. Our life experiences help shape who we are; they tell our stories. Not only of the woman we are in the present moment but also of the woman we are becoming. As women, we can often push down, repress, and suppress our inner wounds; often, the storehouse for these wounds is within the container of our womb. You can imagine what happens over time when the womb is filled with fear and pain and how it can inhibit the full radiant expression of who we are as a woman. Through *Seeds for Tomorrow: How to Access Your Power and Potential to Create Lasting Happiness,* you may commence your journey to step back into the Goddess that has always been a part of your divine feminine essence and live a life in alignment with your soul's purpose.

My life's journey through womanhood has had its heartaches, including a miscarriage and a near-death experience. These traumas and several others along my path have enabled me to learn, grow and evolve as a wife, mother, healer, spiritual teacher and empowered woman in the modern world. I have overcome these challenges and found hope, inner strength, forgiveness and compassion, enabling me to transform these wounds into wisdom restoring harmony and peace within and assisting others to do the same.

The book you are reading has been birthed from the seeds of all my life experiences, including ancestral healing of the mother line for traumas carried within the womb having been passed down through the female lineage contained within the DNA of my body.

While each woman's experiences may differ in content, the fabric is the same in that we each strive to return to a place of divine love of self. I believe the road to finding that deep longing for love is the acceptance of embracing our womb space as a place to nourish, nurture and foster our dreams for a fulfilling life in alignment with the truth of who we really are.

With first-hand personal experience and over two decades of assisting others in coaching and healing the body, mind and spirit, this book is a weaving of all my knowledge and spiritual understanding to this point in my life and to enable women to fully express their gifts of the sacred feminine, which in turn helps raise the consciousness of the planet.

Until we as women understand the enormous power that lies within the female body and start harnessing that power for our highest good, it will be as though we are going through life without the full strength of our inner prowess.

Through *Seeds for Tomorrow: How to Access Your Power and Potential to Create Lasting Happiness,* you will discover and learn practical ways that may enrich your daily life by overcoming obstacles and understanding the rhythms, cycles and phases of life as a glorious woman. It can help women like you rise above the heartache, grief, pain and unworthiness that may be felt at times through life experiences and reconnect to your sacred chalice, opening your feminine pathway to a life of fulfilment.

When you live in alignment with the truth of who you are as a woman, you may use your gifts, talents and abilities to embrace change and genuinely celebrate life in its entirety. This is what happens when you transform wounds into wisdom.

The writing of this book has enabled my soul to bloom, and it is my wish for you that it awakens a deep inner stirring of the ancient Goddess wisdom that dwells inside of you also.

Many blessings from my heart and womb to yours,

Kerry
xx

CHAPTER 1

Wounds of the Womb

"I'm sorry, but there's just no heartbeat." These are the dreaded words every pregnant woman fears hearing. These were the words I heard, and then everything within me turned numb and a sense of emptiness washed over me.

The poet Rumi says that *"The wound is where the light enters you."* Yet, in that period of my life, through the pain, sadness, grief, and heartbreak, little did I know that I was heading toward a significant spiritual awakening.

We store the wounds of our past traumas within each of us. These traumas range in depth but are nevertheless wounds all the same. As women, we often store our wounds within our womb space. The womb is the seat of creation, where we as women birth children, but it is also the birthplace of creativity, where every new idea comes from—every spark, every ignition from within.

As women, we unconsciously push our negative thoughts, feelings and outdated belief patterns down into our womb space. We push down, suppress, and repress our emotions until this sacred space within our bodies becomes clogged with unresolved pain and trauma.

While there may be varying degrees of trauma, and every experience a woman goes through is unique to them, what unites everyone is the emotional pain that is held within. Trauma held within the womb affects the individual woman as opposed to the event itself. The womb can start to feel so painful, perhaps not even physically painful, but heavy, as this is where the energy is trapped. There is then no space to fully evolve as a woman and use our gifts of creativity that we were each innately born with.

Healing our inner wounds is a fundamental need as a woman to learn, grow, and evolve. We need to view our inner wounds as a gift of empowerment, an opportunity to view our lives through a different lens, so that we may courageously step forward instead of being trapped in the past.

The moment you allow yourself to be defined by your wounds, you lose the power to express your full potential. You also lose the ability to see your worth and overcome the obstacles sent to challenge us.

Two people with similar experiences can have a completely different resolve. At the same time, the feelings of grief, pain, loss, sadness, unworthiness and guilt are still experienced by the individual. You are reading this book because you no longer want to allow your inner wounds to destroy you. You no longer want to let these wounds negatively impact your life and your relationships. You are no longer willing to allow these wounds to prevent you from living the fulfilling and joyful life you so deserve.

Having risen from inner wounds that cut so deeply—often crying myself to sleep at night and wondering how I would ever get through the suffering—I understand how challenging it can be. I also know how liberating it is to surrender and release the pain. I've been able to overcome these life challenges and help women like you not only see the silver lining, but also courageously come out on the other side feeling lighter and more at peace and with a greater sense of self-worth.

This book explores many ways to refocus your lens and witness that you can survive and thrive from your deepest inner wound(s), right through to the grazes that merely scratch the surface of your soul. Elevating yourself as a woman in the modern world begins the moment you choose to start.

Many of my past wounds (including pregnancy loss) penetrated so deeply, but in so doing, helped to forge major turning points in my life and created a spiritual awakening, catapulting me on the path of the Goddess. The path of the Goddess being the most empowered version of myself possible. It is time to fully allow the light to enter for every woman on the planet, and that time has never been more needed globally than now.

During the chilling winter of 2007, at the sweet age of twenty-nine, while immersing myself in the beauty of life as a wife with a new home, even a new career, I had just become pregnant with my first child. I was transitioning from my maidenhood (as a young woman full of excitement and enthusiasm for the rich beginnings of life) into the rite of passage of motherhood (with more life responsibilities, including nurturing a new life inside of me). Life was beaming and blossoming around me; I seemingly had it all and did in many ways.

I welcomed the opportunity to become a mother with every fibre of my being. I had a strong desire for a baby for such a long time. I had prepared my womb with energy healing, through my personal meditation and devotional practices, regular chiropractic adjustments, and other health initiatives and regimes.

My chakras were balanced and vibrant; my energy was strong and harmonious. I felt grounded and secure both physically and emotionally. I'd worked hard through meditation and energy healing to help release many fears and feelings of unworthiness, facing my shadow self (the aspects of our personality we generally do not want to accept), and thoughts of feeling not good enough. All my life, I'd sought to feel loved. I came from a loving family home, and while I knew they loved me, I wanted to feel deeply loved by a significant other. I wanted a partner with whom I would share life, love me unconditionally, and create a wonderful family life, and finally, this was coming to fruition.

My energy was flowing freely, and I felt strong within myself. I had detoxed my body and felt that my sacral chakra (the energy centre of the body related to the basis of our emotional well-being) and reproductive organs were now ready for the arrival of a baby who had long been in waiting until I was ready to receive.

In meditation, I had visualised my pregnant belly, I had seen my husband being a proud daddy, and I knew deep within my soul that I would fall pregnant soon. I believe we all strive for the feeling of *wholeness* and *completeness* as women, together with acceptance and belonging, to ourselves and those around us. I remember feeling that having children in my life would bring me that sense of belonging, the opportunity to make me feel whole and complete. I was so ready for pregnancy, and yet my heart had that small reservation of fear that many pregnant mothers have. My husband and I had been married for two years before considering starting a family. When the time finally came, we looked into our fertility and conception health by taking extra vitamins to boost our immune and reproductive systems, alongside other proactive lifestyle choices in the lead up to potential pregnancy.

I desperately wanted everything to be perfect. "I am ready to receive a baby," I would tell myself. "Pregnancy will happen." Positive affirmations flowed into my life. At the time, I didn't know the full intensity of the spoken word or the depth of power and potency of intention setting. The air of pregnancy was all around me. I would see pregnant women in the neighbourhood, in the shops, and on the television; fertility signs were all around me, and it would soon be my turn. The official pregnancy test confirmed my dreams and desires. I was to become a first time mum—I was over the moon! Many couples struggle for years before conception; thankfully, this was not an issue for us. Falling pregnant seemed to occur with a sense of ease.

My soul and the soul of my baby had entwined together, and the sky was the limit for this little one.

My husband and I had gone away for the weekend to the country for a little escape, and that's when the cramping started to happen. Slight cramping is so-called *normal* in pregnancy, so I did my best to breathe through and settle my nervous disposition. "I sleep well at night, and my cramps have ceased," I would tell myself over the next few days. However, not only did the cramps continue when we returned home to the city, but they started to strengthen, and I made an appointment to see my obstetrician. I kept telling myself it would all be okay, yet fears were rising. That is, until I shed blood and could no longer be in denial, I knew something wasn't right.

In a previous appointment with my obstetrician, we heard the beautiful sound of our baby's strong heartbeat. However, this trip to my obstetrician was one of the most challenging times of my life, watching her intently scan my pregnant belly and desperately searching for the heartbeat of my precious little angel. I then knew it was over; my dreams shattered, and my heart ripped in two.

I remember sitting on the steps outside the obstetrician's office and making the devastating call to my mother. Hearing me shakingly voice the words "I lost the baby" out loud was like putting a knife to my heart. I could no longer contain the tears of extreme sorrow; life seemed unfair, and I felt so empty. I wanted the world to swallow me up so I didn't have to feel such excruciating emotional pain. I struggled with intense grief and had no idea how I would survive.

I was determined to become a mother and I was determined to transform these wounds and move forward. I had to find a way to cut through the pain of these wounds and begin to heal from the inside out. By nature, I am optimistic, seeing the glass half full, and I wholeheartedly believe in the body's innate power to heal. While still on maternity leave and having other therapists now working for me in my practice, I continued to focus on working through my grief. The grief process is intimate and unique to each of us, and on the healing journey, we may go through many emotions such as denial, anger, guilt, depression and acceptance. I remember going through all of these and feeling that I would never return to the happy woman I once was.

This wound, while as deep as the ocean, was my way of opening myself to find my *why* here on earth. I didn't know that Heaven would be our baby's forever home. From this day forward, my connection to our unborn son would become my guiding light in the spirit world.

Upon medical advice, it was recommended that three clear menstrual bleeds occur before considering conceiving again. This break allows the uterus to heal, allowing the menstrual cycle to get back on track. Therefore I knew I had three months to get my physical body back in shape and my mental, emotional, and spiritual aspects too; I was determined to do all I could to achieve this.

I've been an avid journal writer since childhood, pouring my desires for the future onto the page and journalling my everyday triumphs and heartaches. Journalling allows you to look back and note the changes in how your thoughts, actions, and beliefs evolve as time goes by. It was a way of releasing what was happening in my head and bringing pen to paper as a means of inner connection.

Confronting my emotions through journalling was a powerful tool in helping me to move forward as I prepared to conceive again. Journalling allowed me the space to pour my heart out, saying words that I was not yet ready to express verbally. My initial journal entries after the miscarriage varied in emotion, but allowed me to express myself without fear. I could write about silent cries in the night, feeling alone. To write about the intensity of excruciating heartache and wanting to scream and howl the place down as opposed to holding back tears of silence.

After miscarriage it's often hard for friends and family to know what to say to you. Sometimes, it's even harder for the partner in the relationship. While both parents suffer the loss and grief of their unborn child, the mother is the one who nurtures the baby growing inside of them. Therefore there is an energetic connection that goes beyond hopes and dreams for the family you are creating. I am not dismissing the grief a partner goes through; merely observing the connection and strands of energy that only a mother herself can experience. It is a bond that enables you to witness how magical the body is in its ability to bring forward new life.

After suffering pregnancy loss, it can be challenging for a woman when others around them are blissfully pregnant. It is often difficult to witness others experiencing joy when you are at the polar opposite end of the spectrum in deep sadness. I also endured this grief while a close girlfriend was heavily pregnant during this challenging phase in my life. She was elated at having a baby (and rightly so) and while I was happy for her, the thought of seeing scanned photos of her unborn child was too much for me to bear at the time.

In addition to sadness, I also experienced feelings of rage. As others questioned why I had my miscarriage, I felt isolated, judged and abandoned. I wondered what on earth I had done to deserve this and where I had gone wrong. I remember journalling about how petrified I was of trying to get pregnant again as I could not endure this pain twice.

By being able to put pen to paper and writing down your inner thoughts, it helps to release the emotional hold a wound has on us as women. It also allows you to express yourself and learn from your experiences. Purchase a beautiful notebook that makes you feel empowered and inspired when you see it, or even use an inexpensive notebook but cover it with pictures or photos that help lift your spirit and raise your vibration. Either way, starting to write your thoughts down is a complete game-changer.

Another cathartic exercise to consider regarding writing and journalling is to express your emotions onto paper and then burn this paper as a powerful ritual. Without holding back, write down all the things you don't feel safe saying aloud. Express your anger, rage, sadness, guilt—whatever it is, write it down, get it out of your head and the storehouse of your womb and release it out of your body.

There is something magical about the element of fire to transform energy. It can be a healing experience to release through fire the thoughts and feelings we hold within us. As the words go up in flames, we can release old wounds and stagnant dreams to prepare ourselves for the journey ahead with a fresh slate and new perspective.

While the trauma I share with you in this chapter relates to my suffering through miscarriage, your wounds may relate to something else entirely. We each experience pain through our wounds and deal with the grief in our own way. Grief is what unites each wound as we embark upon the path to healing.

Use the following as journal prompts in your own situation to help commence the letting go process:
- What emotions am I holding onto from the pain that I wish to release?
- Where am I holding this pain within my body?
- Am I holding on to any resentment toward myself or another?
- What have I learnt about myself from this pain?
- How can I bring more loving kindness to myself as I heal?

Set yourself time regularly (a minimum of once a week) to reflect and tune into your current emotions. When you undertake this kind of exercise, it's best not to try and filter out your words; allow the words to flow onto the paper, knowing that all that has been bottled up inside of you can now be released. Notice your thoughts as you watch the flames rise and how your body— particularly your womb, feels as you use this ritual as a powerful source of healing and transformation. Taking the time to focus on your feelings and how your body responds to stress is vital to healing your wounds and moving forward.

This is an excerpt from a letter I wrote to my little star in Heaven. This letter acted as a gateway for me to start healing my wounds, to let go of the pain, and to focus my intention on clearing my womb for the baby I knew would arrive in divine timing.

While you were only with me for just over 11 weeks, it was the happiest time of my life, you brought me so much joy and I had so many hopes and dreams for our future. You will always be my shining star. My heart aches for you and I feel so lifeless; my eyes are dull and transparent, as though my spirit left along with you. I long for the day, I hold a baby in my arms. For whatever reason you were taken from us, I want you to know that we loved you with all our hearts, we would've given the world to let you be with us. From the moment you were conceived, so much love and warmth surrounded you. I feel such emptiness in my heart now that you are gone. You will forever hold a special place in my heart.

It has been reported that approximately 1 in 4 pregnancies end in miscarriage; this is just one example of the many traumas and wounds a woman may hold within her womb in her lifetime.

You cannot experience the beauty within your essence when you are holding on to the pain of suffering so tightly. This wound of mine cut me to the core, it tested my faith, it tested my sense of belonging, it tested my spiritual beliefs. What did I do wrong? Why did this happen? If there is a God, why did he take our baby away? All of these questions and many more filled my head night and day. I spent several months grieving the loss of our baby and all the hopes and dreams we had as a family. I meditated daily, continued my yoga classes, received energy healing, kept up with my chiropractic adjustments, and processed my emotions (guilt, jealousy, rage, helplessness) through the written word. Another powerful thing was that I gave myself a break by ceasing to berate myself over something out of my control.

I found forgiveness for what was, and accepted that perhaps in this moment I didn't need to understand why it happened and allowed myself to gain strength. I wanted to prepare myself for the little one who was ready to make their journey onto this earth plane, the little one to whom I would be a mother in this lifetime.

Whatever your wounds may be (and as individuals we have many), healing them, releasing them, making peace with yourself and bringing acceptance is a vital component. If we are stuck in the patterns of the past, we cannot move forward.

Without transforming, our wounds inhibit our ability to be who we are and to shine as we were always meant to be, finding the pearls of wisdom from the wound. Through this book, I will help you see that you can move forward in life, just as I have in mine.

Right now, you're feeling the harmful effects of holding onto heartache. You feel you can't let it go, or if you stop grieving, you'll stop caring. These fears and others like them are a natural part of the healing cycle. Take out your journal, think about the aspects of your life and the traumas both big and small that have had an impact upon you and start to notice where the gift is in each wound (there is always a gift, even if we cannot see it at the time). To commence, set aside twenty minutes to start reflecting upon your life and experiences.

- What have been the fundamental causes of stress and trauma in your life?
- What impact did the trauma have upon your health (mentally, emotionally, spiritually as well as physically)?
- What impact did it have on those around you?
- What did you learn about yourself?
- Is there anyone you need to forgive (yourself or another)?
- What are you grateful for?

The last question regarding gratitude can be difficult at first, especially when the emotions are still so raw. However, in every wound there is wisdom, and held within this wisdom is a form of gratitude for the experience and what it has taught you.

I know how hard it can be to find peace with some of the devastating things that can happen to us as women, but if you can honour yourself by taking the time to think back on your wounds and find the wisdom you gained, you begin to free yourself from suffering. You are worthy of this freedom, and looking at the wisdom you have gained from all you have endured is an enormous step forward and one you can be proud of yourself for.

The womb space is one place within the body where we store energetic imprints of emotional memories, past relationships, lovers, unresolved pain and trauma. It is also the space to store deep wisdom and creative power, from which all our seeds of inspiration come, as well as to birth children (if that is our calling in this lifetime). The womb space enables us to create, and one of my greatest passions in life is to help women connect to their womb and to heal the wounds held within this sacred container.

While studying in California at Denise Linn's gorgeous Star Mountain Ranch, I was fortunate to have received the 13th Rite of the Munay-Ki from a fellow Red Lotus® sister. The 13th Rite of the Munay-Ki is an energetic transmission received from a lineage of women deep in the jungle of Peru. This lineage of women freed themselves from suffering, and they want us all to remember:

"The womb is not a place to store fear and pain; the womb is to create and to give birth to life."

(13th Rite of the Munay-Ki)

I am now one of many womb keepers across the globe who regularly gifts this rite to women so that they may also receive it and start their own personal healing journey. After receiving this rite of the womb (the nurturing energetic transmission) you are able to share this transmission forward to others by facilitating a womb rite ceremony. This transmission releases fear and pain held within the womb space and allows for birthing new life and creative endeavours. In receiving the rite, women can witness the sacredness within them and life as a whole.

When a woman heals her womb, she in turn heals her mother, her sister, her daughter and ultimately Mother Earth—the lakes, rivers, streams and oceans she embodies within sacred waters across the globe.

Holding onto and storing our pain serves nobody, least of all ourselves. Each wound serves as a way to open ourselves to our greatness and learn our strengths and endurance level. To learn about what it is we are willing to accept in life and what it is we wish to surrender and let go of.

The inner wound I received through miscarriage was one of the most heartbreaking experiences of my life, and yet it was in the cracking open of my heart that I allowed the light in. This experience taught me so much; it taught me about love, loss, and the power to ultimately heal from the inside out, while enhancing my intuitive abilities. I can now reflect on this turning point in my life with deep gratitude. While I do believe that you do not necessarily have to suffer to grow, sometimes it is our destiny to endure certain suffering to expand our consciousness and how we view our life and the choices we make moving forward. Life may not always seem fair, but if you allow yourself to remain in victim mode mentality (e.g. feeling that things will never change or get better) this keeps you in a state of suffering instead of seeing how you may grow from your experience.

Throughout my time as a coach, healer and spiritual teacher, I have gathered much insight and multiple skills within my toolkit to help clients and myself. Quite often as healers, we attract clients who may have walked similar paths or perhaps had similar experiences, especially in the field of energy work. While we help others to heal, we heal ourselves in the process (we are all continuously in a state of growth, peeling back the layers and healing from the inside out). A part of my healing journey took me down the path of training with Denise Linn at her *Women's Mystery School*, learning the way of the Goddess and the wild woman within. This then led me to train back home in Australia as a Womb & Fertility Practitioner, further enhancing my connection to the womb as a source of healing.

I have found through my clinical practice over the years that it is pretty common that the word *womb* has a negative connotation for many women, and it is a word many women certainly don't like to use, let alone connect with. A part of this could be because they have had a difficult time through menstruation, or feel a disconnect between themselves and this area of the female body due to a past trauma or beliefs. Many women only see its significance during pregnancy. They do not have an understanding of the complexity of its power.

Start to view your womb as your personal sacred chalice, and see it as a vessel that has the power to bring new life into this world and bring new life to yourself through ideas and creative endeavours. Part of this connection is finding a way to understand this sacred part of your anatomy (so that you may fully access your inner feminine power), and to find a way for you to connect with it so that the word womb is seen as one of beauty, of honour, of grace and of womanly wisdom.

The womb and the uterus are two commonly referred-to features of a woman's body, and the main difference between them is in each part's role. The female reproductive system comprises the vagina, cervix, uterus, fallopian tubes and ovaries (refer to Female Reproductive System diagram).

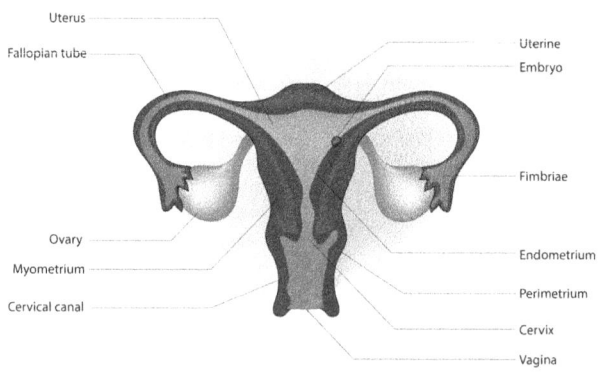

Female Reproductive System

The womb is the organ through which a baby is conceived and matured until birth, so most textbooks only use the term *womb* throughout pregnancy. The uterus is the major organ of the female reproductive system in which the fertilised egg is implanted. Throughout pregnancy, the womb consists of the developing child, placenta and umbilical cord. The uterus, on the other hand, consists of three layers: the endometrium (the inner layer of the uterus), myometrium (middle layer) and perimetrium (outer layer). From a functional perspective, the womb provides nutrients and support to the developing embryo. In contrast, the uterus provides space for the implantation of the fertilised egg.

Within this book, I refer to *womb* as the sacred container into which a woman may access creativity, whether for the procreation of children or manifesting ideas of the heart. It is the energetic centre of consciousness.

It is also important to note energetically that you still have a womb if you have had a hysterectomy. In many respects, it can be alikened to the "phantom missing limb pain" that has been described when amputees continue to experience sensations from a limb after it has been removed. From an energetic perspective, this limb remains and so does the energetic connection to your womb space post-hysterectomy.

Through negative thought patterns and outdated beliefs, we inadvertently give the power of our womb away by subconsciously storing our inner wounds. The feminine wisdom and power is always accessible and available; however it may be somewhat hidden, and therefore it is vital that you are able to reconnect with this sacred container in order to reclaim your feminine wisdom and inner power fully.

The next exercise will help you begin to connect with your womb as your sacred chalice and keeper of your feminine wisdom and inner power.

Womb Connection

Find yourself a quiet place to sit or lie down where you will not be disturbed and can allow yourself to relax. Soothing music in the background may help you unwind, or allow yourself to tune in to the sounds of your natural environment.

Once you are comfortable, gently and lovingly place your hands in the form of a triangle over your womb space (position thumbs together and then pointer fingers together with the rest of the fingers laying comfortably over the abdominal and womb region, refer to diagram below).

Womb Meditation Pose

- Close your eyes and take several relaxing, slow and deep breaths into your body.
- Connect to your breath. Slowly breathe out and release.
- Breathe in deeply and fully.
- Notice how your belly rises and falls as you breathe and also the way your chest expands.
- Breathe in deeply and fully.
- Connect to the rhythm of your heart.
- Slowly breathe out and release.

Notice and recognise your thoughts and feelings, and also what your heart space needs (the non-physical part, the essence of who you are) and wants from you energetically; permit yourself to really feel your emotions.

- Breathe in deeply and fully.
- Connect to your womb space.
- Slowly breathe out and release.
- Think of your womb space as a cup filling with love and acceptance through your breath as if it's liquid light.

As you connect deeper and deeper, bringing your awareness and focus to your womb area with every breath, ask yourself, "*What is my womb's message for me today?*" Listen for the answer from within without judgment—allow the words to flow. There is always a message inside of us. Sometimes they are whispers from the soul, and sometimes they are loud resounding bellows. The message you receive is valid; trust what comes through without judgment. Even if you feel you are making it up, go with what comes through; your imagination is often what opens the doorway to further insights. When you step out of your head space and into your heart and womb space, this is where you hear the voice of your soul.

After your connection, take out your journal and note down the answers and wisdom you received; even the smallest insight can hold immense wisdom. Make it a regular practice, setting aside time to meditate with a journal nearby. You will be amazed at how much insight starts to pour forward when you commit to even 5-10 minutes a day to switch off your mind's thinking mode and step into the feeling mode of your womb.

The exercise above is a simple, yet a profoundly powerful exercise in womb connection. Create time and space to connect to your womb regularly. You will find that your intuitive messages start to deepen and your connection to your womb grows stronger. Use this method as a form of daily ritual to connect to your womb each morning upon waking, or as a final connection before sleep at night. It doesn't have to take a long time to connect, however you will benefit by feeling more grounded and centred, and notice a greater sense of self-awareness that goes beyond the physical body.

Regular womb connection through the breath will help transform negative emotional experiences and promote a healthier relationship to self and others by bringing more unconditional love, ultimately leading you to a sense of freedom to create space for new beginnings.

Undertaking the exercise will allow you to bring focus, intention and awareness into your own personal sacred chalice. Your womb is the storehouse of all that you wish to create in this world. Cherish the time you spend connecting regularly, and start honouring the beauty you hold within, no matter what is happening around you.

Over the years, I have discovered many methods that helped me on my wound and womb healing journey, shifting from pain to joy. Throughout this book, I share these tools with you so that you may heal alongside me.

Aromatherapy Connection

My love for aromatherapy has been with me since I was a teenager when I first learned about skin care routines. I lovingly recall my mother and I receiving self-care using beauty therapy treatments that often incorporated aromatherapy. It always ignited a sense of joy and excitement within me. An opportunity to tune out from the busyness of the world around me and tune inward where there is always peace and stillness.

I remember collecting my first set of essential oils and it bringing back memories of lifetimes throughout Egypt and beyond where I created lotions, potions and elixirs for medicinal healing purposes and beauty needs for myself and those in my care.

I worked for ten years in the fast-paced corporate world before I embarked upon a career in natural therapies. Aromatherapy was one of the first modalities I wanted to study when going into the field of massage therapy. I found that aromatherapy's healing benefits for body, mind and soul was a wonderful stress release from the hustle and bustle within the legal industry. Since then, the powerful uses of essential oils has become a means to help me relax. Gaining my aromatherapy diploma has been one of the many highlights of my life. As a Soul Coaching® Practitioner, I also weave my knowledge of using aromatherapy to connect further with nature and in the practice of Elemental Space Clearing®.

When it comes to healing the wounds of the womb as a woman, from an energetic perspective, using essential oils is a wonderful way in which to explore the scents that evoke our womanly senses.

An exquisite essential oil to choose to honour yourself as a woman is that of rose essential oil. I cannot think of a more beautiful essential oil to reflect the beauty inside and out than rose essential oil. Symbolically, the rose blooming throughout all stages of life can also be used to correspond to the phases and stages we go through as a woman being that of maiden, mother, maga and crone.

Many women struggle with appreciating their physical body, particularly through the ageing process, when perhaps their body is no longer as supple as it once was or they are going through a particularly difficult time in their life emotionally.

A powerful self-care and self-love ritual using essential oils is to incorporate aromatic dressing. This helps bring more self-confidence and self-esteem toward yourself and towards appreciating your body.

I love to set my intentions for the day ahead using aromatic dressing after showering in the morning or as a means to give gratitude for the day's experiences after showering in the evening (plus, it's a beautiful way to moisturise and nourish your skin in the process).

As you massage the oils into your body, use this opportunity to affirm positive things toward your body. Using big sweeping motions across your body parts, you can say something to yourself such as "I'm grateful for my strong legs, supporting me on my adventures". Focus on your abdomen (including your womb), which is often an area of the body that women can think quite negatively toward. Use this time to say uplifting things like "I love and appreciate my belly and all the ways it enables me to create", as you connect to your body and all your beautiful womanly curves. If you have any visible scars on your body it is a great opportunity to connect and say, "I love and appreciate my scars". This is a powerful means to acknowledge that, while you and your body may have been through some difficult times, you draw upon your inner strength and use it to remind yourself that you are worthy of love.

As I mentioned above, I love rose essential oil, and women of all ages can use it as a reminder of the most important love there is, the love of self.

What you will need:
- 2 tablespoons of carrier oil of your choice (e.g. almond oil)
- 6 drops of rose essential oil
- 1 small bowl

Dip your fingers in a small bowl and apply the oil with love and gratitude to your entire body.

Using the above self-care ritual is a beautiful way of enhancing your mood and also creating positive body image awareness.

Crystal Connection

I am passionate about working with crystals, particularly when it comes to connecting to the womb space. The stone carnelian is an essential stone within the crystal kingdom for women.

From a metaphysical perspective, carnelian can help balance a woman's reproductive system, including the ovaries, fallopian tubes, uterus, cervix and vagina. In many respects, the colour and energy of this stone is powerfully aligned to that of a woman's womb. The rich fiery orange and brownish-red colours can be associated with our menstrual bleed.

Carnelian corresponds to the lower three chakras, which are spinning wheels of energy within the physical and ethereal body (root: located at the very base of the spine, sacral: located in the lower abdomen, just below the naval, and solar plexus: located just below the rib cage). These lower three chakras are crucial for our ability to feel grounded and have solid foundations to grow spiritually, mentally, emotionally, and physically.

Over the years, whilst working with my womb and fertility clients, I have highly recommended the crystal carnelian due to its healing properties pertaining to the reproductive system. When it comes to healing the wounds of the womb, there is another crystal that every woman can benefit from: the ever-beautiful and loving rose quartz (similarly to rose essential oil, the gift of self-love from this crystal is exponential).

Using both carnelian and rose quartz together is a powerful combination toward energetically helping to bring in both self-love and deeper awareness to the heart and the womb space together.

Working with the above crystals in your daily meditation practice, and incorporating it with the womb connection exercise mentioned previously, will bring you vitality and self-love.

In meditation, place the rose quartz lovingly upon your heart chakra (located in the centre of your chest) and the carnelian at your sacral chakra (located just below your belly button) and gently allow it to rest upon your womb.

Visualise these crystals healing the wounds within you and allowing the energy of the crystals to weave their healing powers into your body.

Your crystals must be cleansed and cleared regularly while you're using them to heal your inner wounds. You may do this by placing your crystals out in the sunlight or moonlight to recharge, cleansing them under running water (although some crystals are water-soluble and cannot be cleansed with water as they will be damaged e.g. selenite), using sound instruments, or smudging them with sage or palo santo.

Goddess Connection

There are many Goddess energies that you may choose to assist you throughout womanhood and toward transforming your wounds into wisdom.

One of my favourites is the ancient Egyptian Goddess Isis, known as a Goddess of magic, fertility, motherhood, death and rebirth.

After our miscarriage, my husband and I went on a life-changing trip throughout Egypt. My time in Egypt was rich in ancient wisdom and awe-inspiring spiritual moments of deep inner discovery. It was in Egypt, particularly upon the River Nile, that I first developed my connection to this powerful Goddess.

Another Egyptian Goddess who made herself known to me throughout our stay in these ancient lands was that of Hathor, who is a Goddess of the sky, women, fertility and love. Given that Hathor, much like Isis, is a Goddess of motherhood, it was a vital component to help me connect deeply with my womb, (although I didn't know this at the time). It was as though both of these powerful Goddess energies infused together to help me prepare my womb, firstly to soothe the sorrow held within from the miscarriage, and then help heal and create space for the baby who would arrive soon after. My connection to Goddess Hathor acted as an initiation of sorts, bringing me back to my ancient roots and reclaiming the power of the Goddess within me.

In many respects, this trip throughout Egypt was like a re-birthing experience. I recall cruising along the River Nile, reflecting upon the sadness endured as a former mother-to-be and the feelings of loss and grief that still stirred within my heart, soul and womb space. At the same time, I was filled with hope and excitement, for I truly believed that a baby, who I would soon hold in my arms, was to make its entrance in the time ahead. Perhaps more than I realised at the time, Goddess Isis had her part to play in this encapsulating adventure.

I was releasing and letting go of one child and welcoming in the energies of another. Looking at our inner wounds is often a re-birthing experience as we make our way across the threshold, having released what no longer serves us and looking back at the wisdom gained along the way.

During this trip, I visited many ancient and sacred sites. I felt as though I had visited many of these sites before. It was like an ancient remembering for me of past initiations I received as a high priestess in past lifetimes spent here. Further within this book we explore, in more depth various archetypes we exude as women (including that of the high priestess). Many of the experiences I've had, particularly over the last couple of decades, have been so that I may assist women toward reclaiming their divine feminine essence. Every land I have ever touched has remained within me; equally, I have also left a part of me upon those lands. This is a fair exchange between myself and Mother Earth. She gifts me her wisdom to infuse within me and to impart upon others, while I give love from my heart and my womb back into the womb of the great mother herself.

One Egyptian temple with a particularly strong embodiment within me is the Temple of Philae in Aswan, also known as the Temple of Isis. Philae was an important centre of worship for Goddess Isis, and remained this way long after Christianity took hold across the Mediterranean.

During our time in Egypt, we had many interesting spiritual encounters, including a powerful experience at the Valley of the Kings near Luxor, where King Tutankhamun's tomb resides. One of the male ticket guides at the entrance of this sacred site referred to needing a ticket for the "baby" and gave me a knowing smile.

Looking back upon that now, it could be seen as two things: that this Egyptian local could sense the energy of the baby we lost through miscarriage, or he was sensing the energy of the baby (our daughter to be, Cara) who was to embody my womb in the weeks to come. Perhaps he was also sensing both children's energies. All I know is that it was a sign from above that my womb was indeed ready to again receive, and that seeds of creation were to be born.

No man made structure in the world holds as much mystery as the Great Pyramid. This was yet another powerful memory of our time in Egypt. We excitedly made our way up the narrow space of the tight ascending passageway to the Kings Chamber where King Khufu's granite sarcophagus rests. There have been many theories over the years that the Egyptian pyramids are a gateway to the stars. All I know is that as I lay within this granite sarcophagus, I felt a surge of power fill from within. Whether the alignment of the stars, the constellation Orion and its correlation to the Giza Pyramids is fact or fiction remains to be seen, however this energy and power still rises within me whenever I think about it.

Our wounds enable us to heal as time goes on, together with focused action to let go of the pain and turn it into aspects of inner growth. Regarding our womb space, as women, we can draw upon our own internal power to help channel the energy within to release those feelings that are often submerged and suppressed. In turn, we enable an expansion of possibilities moving forward.

We can work alongside Goddess energies such as Isis and Hathor to assist us throughout various phases of womanhood, especially through meditation where we call upon them specifically for assistance. Another Goddess you may wish to connect with is that of the Mayan Goddess Ix-Chel. She is the Goddess of the moon, water, childbirth, fertility, creativity and rebirth.

I first connected with this particular Goddess in San Gervasio, Cozumel. This Goddess has qualities both of a young, sensual woman, and that of a wise old crone. Women worldwide have gathered as pilgrims to the Ix-Chel shrine that I visited in Cozumel (a Mexican Island in the Caribbean Sea) which has specific celestial alignments with the moon. Typically, most tourists find their way to Cozumel on cruise ships (like I did), however many don't find their way to this particular shrine.

In true form, throughout my life I have often found myself in places across the globe that are off the beaten track, or perhaps not somewhere that the average tourist would find themselves in. While I may not always understand why at the time, these global sites always make themselves known in divine timing. I often like to think of it as my own re-initiation into lands of old that have wisdom to share with me. The heart of this wisdom sits within my womb space, gestating until the time is right to bear fruit with these insights for the greater good of all. The womb is a sacred, powerful seat of creativity for every woman, and the ability to access this wisdom opens when we choose to receive.

As you develop your connection with various Goddess energies and the qualities they have to offer, you may notice where you have these same attributes and enhance these aspects within yourself. Hathor, Isis and Ix-Chel are just a few examples of a Goddess for fertility, childbirth, creativity and rebirth. Remembering that the term *birth* explores aspects of what we are bringing forward into the world other than children alone. There are many more with whom you may explore your own connection. Allow your womb to be your guide; you may wish to create a monthly ritual whereby you seek to connect to a different Goddess and explore the attributes she has to offer which in turn correlate to your own life as a woman. I have done this for many years in women's circles, and each woman has grown exponentially due to these deep connections and Goddess discoveries.

Meditation is a key element of the healing work I suggest you undertake. Creating an altar nearby your meditation space is a powerful tool when healing our unresolved pain stored in the womb. It doesn't need to be large—a small table or even a part of a bookshelf will suffice. What it brings is a distinct representation of you and your hopes and dreams to heal and move forward. Creating an altar also helps to define your space, bringing you a central focal point in which to keep building upon the energy of a particular Goddess and intention.

Goddess Isis is frequently depicted wearing the horns of a cow. Therefore, noticing milk as you go about your day is a beautiful way of bringing recognition to this Goddess. Adding a drop of milk to your morning tea or coffee can bring your awareness to Goddess Isis personally, thanking her for the wisdom and magic she shares with you. Milk, honey and flowers are traditional offerings to Isis to consider placing on your altar.

Call upon Goddess Isis when you require her magic gifts in problem solving and to experience the joys of motherhood and fertility (the nurturing of either a baby or a project).

Similarly to Goddess Isis, Hathor is associated with milk; hence, offerings of milk on an altar are welcomed by her, along with beer, copper or turquoise items. The wearing of makeup is also strongly related with her, therefore when you apply your makeup you may acknowledge her presence within your life and apply with specific intentions to invoke her.

Another way to invoke Hathor in your life is to use the art of gratitude. There is an ancient Egyptian ritual called *The Five Gifts of Hathor*. As you lay in bed at the end of the day, on one hand count five things you are grateful for (naming anything you hold close to your heart). This will also help open your heart toward appreciating all areas of your life, despite any hardship an inner wound may hold within you.

The Egyptians believed that your heart needed to be as light as a feather at the time of death in order to lead to eternal life. The Five Gifts of Hathor are a way to bring balance and harmony into your life. It's a beautiful way to see how bringing the Goddess into your life and your home can enrich your life as a woman in the modern world, just like those of the ancients.

Earlier in this chapter, one of the questions we explored was what we are grateful for regarding our inner wounds. Incorporating the Five Gifts of Hathor ritual into your life can help you see the silver linings within every situation throughout womanhood.

Call upon Goddess Hathor to bring joy and celebration to your life, particularly when you seek more inspiration. She can also help you boost your self-esteem when you are feeling at a low ebb.

Goddess Ix-Chel is known as the *Lady of the Rainbow*, and burning candles in various colours upon your altar is a beautiful way to honour her. Using the juice or seeds of pomegranate in a bowl on an altar is another way to honour her. Chocolate is another way to honour her, so when you next taste that delicious bite of velvety chocolate in your mouth, think of this powerful Mayan Goddess and her powers of creativity and fertility. The Mayans believed the cacao bean held magical powers.

Goddess Ix-Chel is often pictured with a rabbit (a well-known symbol of fertility) and is a symbol the Mayans saw in the face of the moon. I recall it being the full moon while at Star Mountain Ranch in California for my Red Lotus training. It was here that I was first made aware of the *rabbit in the moon* concept (illuminated within the full moon is an image of a rabbit). This may be new to you also; therefore the next time it's a full moon, I invite you to step outside and look up to Grandmother Moon's illuminating light for the rabbit in the moon and think of Goddess Ix-Chel. The full moon is a time of release and letting go of the things that no longer serve you. Goddess Ix-Chel is a wonderful Goddess to call upon when letting go of something (e.g. inner wounds) to make room for new energy to enter.

To evoke a particular Goddess such as the ones mentioned above, prior to settling down for meditation you may silently say:

"I hereby call upon Goddess (insert name of the Goddess e.g. Isis) and ask that she assist me with aspects of fertility in regard to (insert your specific need relating to the birth of beginnings) in my life."

Be sure to thank her afterwards for her assistance and note any wisdom received, or how you felt during meditation in your journal. Writing down your thoughts and feelings is a powerful way of also developing your strength and personal connection to a particular Goddess.

Affirmation

Using affirmations can be a great way to inspire your connection to your womb space daily to help overcome self-sabotage and negative thought patterns. Repeat the affirmation at the conclusion of each chapter several times throughout the day to deepen your personal womb connection.

"My womb is a sacred vessel for creation."

Seed #1

Connect into your past wounds, knowing that all that has occurred in the past does not define who you are as a woman. In every moment, we have the opportunity to witness our wounds and transform them into pearls of wisdom for our future. Use your life's turning points to discover a way forward that supports your future self's success.

Your womb is the sacred container of creation for which you ignite a life of passion, purpose and self-empowerment.

CHAPTER 2

Cycling Towards Empowerment

I listened intently with eyes wide open, new information was filtering through as I sat with quiet apprehension mixed with a little spice of excitement for what lay ahead. It was during the commencement of a brand new school year being the summer of 1990 and the girls were sent off in one class and the boys in another. It all felt very secretive and a little mysterious, the discussion in this lesson was on the changes taking place within the female body and our impending time ahead for menstruation.

It was a very quiet, emotionless and structured discussion that left us as young girls feeling a little mystified, wondering what it was going to be like. Would it rush like a tap and have us embarrassed in the classroom upon standing? Would it hurt? What are people going to say when they find out? All of these random thoughts were entering my head and I'm sure I wasn't alone. We were all headed into foreign territory, wondering what lay ahead for us. Our school created a big "red box" (not exactly discreet!) so that if we were caught out unprepared with our period occurring at school, we were to discretely, yet with a sense of urgency head to the front office and ask for the "red box". I mean really? Can you imagine anything more daunting for a young girl than to scurry down to the front office not knowing if there was a trail of destruction behind and to ask for this whopping great big red box full of unknown foreign goods to mop up the embarrassing mess we'd somehow created! Well, those were the daunting thoughts racing around in my mind in those primary school days.

The year went by and soon enough school was out for another year and summer holidays had commenced at long last. Freedom and fun were within my grasp. Camping holidays at Christmas, soaking up the summer sunshine, life as a young girl was carefree. I was 12 years old and heading toward my 13th birthday at the end of that summer.

As it happened, I didn't receive my first bleed in primary school and so avoided the whole scenario of the "red box" situation. Instead for me, my first bleed came just prior to me starting high school, literally the very first day (talk about a rite of passage!). To be honest I can't really recall my feelings at the time, it's all a bit of a blur, but I do know that it wasn't as bad as I was expecting. I think perhaps I was pre-occupied with the hype and prospect of starting a new school, so therefore having my period was secondary to my greater concerns and focus at that specific point in my life.

I was fortunate to have had a blessed experience throughout my early menstruating years and didn't suffer from excruciating menstrual pain like some of my friends. The formal discussion on periods wasn't as openly discussed back then. I remember my mum handing me a booklet to read that she'd probably kept for years in the lead up, she bought me my supplies each month and that was the end of that. I don't even recall chatting to my girlfriends at the time about it very much either. What we learned; we learned out of magazines. Here in Australia it was either the *Dolly* magazine or *Girlfriend* magazine that Australian teenage girls would read on a regular basis and therefore what we learned about life as a teenager was through these articles (some of which looking back were probably less than appropriate). In many respects these days the internet has taken over from any unanswered questions, although I would like to think that young women entering menarche today have an exposure that is more open, kind, educational and holistic in nature.

I feel that we have come such a long way in respect to the information that is out there today for young women entering menarche. Plus, there is a lean toward a more open attitude about menstruation and discussing the changes within a woman's body. It is becoming less about hiding and placing items in the bottom of our grocery trolley (heaven forbid that anybody would see) and more about it being a healthy fact of life. The more we can encourage our daughters (and daughters of friends) to experience a positive outlook toward their bleed, the more open we become as a society to incorporate the menstrual cycle into the daily lives of women without shame, guilt, fear and negativity attached. These negative emotions again sit in the container of a woman's womb, inhibiting her sense of freedom and creative expression.

I truly believe that one of the reasons that I bore a daughter into this world at this time on the planet is so that I could have the opportunity to witness and take part in a new thought paradigm. An opportunity to learn from my own past experiences and to share new ones in a more fulfilling light with a future generation. A generation that honours the receiving of her menstrual bleed each month and works toward seeing that our menstrual cycle isn't just one week a month, but that our cycle incorporates an entire month of physical, physiological, emotional and spiritual changes that occur and keeps evolving much like nature does around us. As a woman our menstrual cycle follows a similar pattern and rhythm that nature does. The shedding each month is akin to the leaves falling off the trees in autumn and going inward during winter ahead of the more outward, expressive seasons to follow.

Throughout a woman's menstrual cycle we go through various emotions, i.e. the rises and falls of being. Sometimes you feel upbeat, as if you could literally take on the world and other times you want to curl up in a ball, pull the covers over your head and shut the world out. All of these ways of being are justified and valid but when you understand the meanings behind the feelings and become more in sync with our own rhythm and flow we begin to be able to work alongside our cycle and become more in flow with life overall.

For me, the art of cycle syncing didn't really become a ritual on a regular basis until I was looking at falling pregnant and then more deeply when I became a womb and fertility practitioner. Although, I recall from an early age I used to track my cycle so that I would know when my menstrual cycle was due, I only ever did it as a means of knowing when to be prepared for bleeding. These days however there is so much more that I understand about how tracking your cycle can benefit you for the entire month, not just as a means of an alarm clock prior to your bleed.

There is also great irony in the fact that many of us have been brought up with the thought process that in our early menstruating years we dread the thought of receiving our period as it inhibits our lifestyle or we are most definitely not looking to fall pregnant. Then there is the phase of a woman's life when if she does wish to fall pregnant, every time she receives her bleed it can often be seen as a failure and missed opportunity for those on the fertility path toward child rearing. This may also be the case when a woman heads toward the changes taking place during menopause and beyond it is a reminder of the ageing process.

If only we were taught at school the ability to honour our womanly cycle more than simply an education in scientific facts of menstruation and having a baby, through the participation in a biology class, our perception on menstruation would be vastly different. If we were taught about being able to view our menstrual bleed as a gift each month including how to track our cycle along the way to assist us with our health and wellbeing, as well as how to use our cycle for productivity and empowerment, then our level of awareness and understanding of life as a woman would be exponential. Hopefully in the years to follow this trend can become fact. The rites of passage from menarche, to motherhood and menopause is one of honour and wisdom and we as a society need to return to the ways of our ancestors to reclaim this. A woman's bleed is one of the most natural states of the female body and it should be treated with the utmost respect.

If you are still receiving your bleed there is no greater time than now to dive deep into the discovery of who you are as a woman and activate your menstrual power. Or, if on the other hand, you are a woman who has reached the time of menopause and/or no longer receive your bleed, do not despair, you may follow the light of the moon to chart your course throughout the month. You may also like to give yourself an opportunity to perhaps reflect and journal on the ways that various times during your monthly cycle would make you feel. This is the beauty of being a woman and being able to connect with the natural rhythms of life, be it our internal rhythm or our external rhythm, ultimately the two are majestically entwined and bring rich wisdom into our lives.

Typically, the average menstrual cycle for a woman is twenty eight days. This is similar to the calendar month and so we can divide the month into four categories.

Days 1-7 (Bleeding, Inner Winter)

Days 8-14 (Pre-Ovulation, Inner Spring)

Days 15-21 (Ovulation, Inner Summer)

Days 22-28 (Pre-Menstruum, Inner Autumn)

There are of course what is known as *cross over days* where one season starts to merge and blend with the next. Often a woman may feel a little out of sorts during the cross over or extremely intuitive, every woman varies with her approach to her unique cycle.

Let's journey through the monthly cycle to get a feel for its potential power.

Days 1-7 of the cycle is when a woman receives her bleed. So often throughout our modern age women have been known to groan at the prospect of the arrival of her period. It has been seen as a hindrance, an ogre, a punishment of sorts and society has come to see it as nothing more than a pain (and for some women it can be a physical pain and I am in no way diminishing this fact, although there is always a deep rooted message from the body behind this physical pain). When you start to connect with your bleed and understand what happens throughout the month from a spiritual and emotional perspective, rather than simply a physiological perspective you begin to have a greater appreciation for the expansiveness and wisdom that each week provides.

This is the time of the month when hormone levels are at their lowest and therefore energy levels can often take a dip at this time. Then as the bleed comes to an end it then allows for oestrogen levels to rise which brings with it the feel good attitude. The light at the end of the tunnel.

The first 7 days are an opportunity for us as women to retreat to the quiet place within. Similarly, if you can think about how you feel during the time of winter when typically, you want to retreat inside, and hibernate. This is exactly what women used to do in times of old (refer to chapter 5, The Way of the Ancients for further information) as women would gather in Red Tents or Moon Lodges away from the routines of everyday life to retreat with their women elders for rest and nurturing. This is a powerful time of intuitive abilities and a time when solitude and listening to the inner stirrings of the soul is heightened and we can often want to detach ourselves from the outside world. The time of winter is a beautiful opportunity for us to plant the seeds of our intentions within the fertile soil of our soul in preparedness for the time ahead. It is also a wonderful opportunity for us to gift ourselves the further act of self-care and bring more self-love into our lives. As women we can so often be over giving and yet when it comes time for us to receive it is not as easy. However there needs to be giving and receiving in equal proportions in order for you to fully thrive toward your greatest potential both as a woman and in life's pursuits overall.

During this phase of the month, both the left and right brain hemispheres are communicating so much more powerfully across the corpus collosum and you are able to access both the intuitive aspects as well as your analytical aspects to your greatest advantage.

During your time in winter I suggest that you ask yourself the following questions:

1. What does my body need from me right now?
2. What acts of self-love can I receive?
3. Where can I schedule time in my life to adequately rest?
4. What is it that I wish to create in the month to follow?

Affirmation for winter:
> *"I nurture my body through rest, so that I may emerge from my cocoon, as the beautiful butterfly that I am."*

When you commence viewing your bleed as an opportunity to let go and surrender to the act of nourishment, self-love, rest and give yourself the space for quiet time, it brings a sense of wondrous beauty to this sacred time in a woman's month. If society were to bring awareness to this aspect, we can begin to create change and the younger generation may be enabled to honour their bleed like those of our ancestors. There is rich wisdom to be found if you only allow yourself to slow down and listen to the rhythm and flow of your womanly body.

Days 8-14 of our cycle are much like a burst of fresh air. We have completed our bleed time and are now ready to greet the world with excitement. If you are a dog lover like me, I think of spring time much like when you return home at the end of a long day and they are there excitedly wagging their tails, ever so pleased to see you. Or the feeling of being able to experience the sunshine on your face after a long and wet winter. It's the overwhelming feeling of *I can do anything* that this phase of our cycle brings. It is a time when motivation is at its peak and you are laser focused upon your goals. From a physiological perspective the time of spring is our pre-ovulatory phase.

While there is this air of excitement during this phase, this is also a time to ease back into life with a little caution. After all, you have just spent the previous week in nurture and rest mode, going full out too soon can deplete your resources. Therefore, it is best to be gentle as you come out of your cocooned life and while you may have a surge of energy you also need to consider giving yourself time to emerge on your terms.

During your time in spring I suggest that you ask yourself the following questions:

1. What did I learn from my week of rest?
2. How can I enter back into the world at a slower pace?
3. Where can I focus my enthusiasm for life?
4. What can I do to bring more play into my week?

Affirmation for spring:
"My life is filled with boundless opportunities and I pause to consider my direction."

Days 15-21 of a woman's cycle can often be the most glorious. This is the time of our inner summer, the time when a woman may often feel her most radiant. Think about the depths of summer and how your body glows with a warm sense of fun, adventure and living life to the maximum. This is the feeling of your time during ovulation. When you think about it from a physiological perspective this is the time frame where if there was ever going to be a fertilised egg and the prospective birth of a new little person, it is now. Therefore, whether you are looking to birth the creation of a child or a creative endeavour, this is the time to surge forward, the time is now!

Your energy levels are at their peak and you are a woman of strength, power and the ability to take charge of your world with optimistic magnetism. It's often a time when you are at your most social too and you love and appreciate all that your glorious life has to offer. Those who are in your company at this phase are likely to feel uplifted around you as you bloom beyond comparison.

During your time in summer I suggest that you ask yourself the following questions:
1. How can I step out more boldly into the world with all that I have to offer?
2. What brings me joy and how can I achieve more of this?

3. Where can I make time in my schedule to be more social this week?
4. Where do I need to focus my attention to get jobs done?

Affirmation for summer:
"My life brings me pleasure and I bring immense joy wherever I go."

Days 22-28 of a woman's cycle is typically the most challenging one in terms of being misunderstood. For many women this time of autumn during our pre-menstruum is often given a bad reputation. It's the "have you got PMT?" or "boy, are you little Miss Cranky Pants today!" or the "just leave me alone" emotional rantings. All of these and many other similar lines can often come up during this phase of a woman's cycle. From a physiological perspective the hormonal changes during this phase can result in women experiencing changes in mood as well as bloating, breast tenderness, acne and other symptoms due to a drop in oestrogen and progesterone levels in preparation for shedding during the next menstrual bleed to follow.

While all of the above may seem like less than a bundle of fun, there is great wisdom to come from this phase of the cycle. The time of autumn brings with it an awareness of our shadow side. Often we can prefer to be in our light but as with everything in life we need our light and our shadow in order to function at our optimum and be in a state of balance.

This phase gives us an opportunity to bring awareness to the things you have been putting off and to acknowledge what you are ready to let go of in life. It's often a time that you as a woman can be the hardest on yourself and so watching your self-talk is crucial and bringing yourself into alignment with the real truth of your situation.

When it comes to your womb space this is your seat of creativity and it's often during this particular phase of the month that women may feel the urge to be more creative and your intuitive abilities are also heightened. The whole act of being a little more sensitive during this time of the menstrual cycle can be viewed upon as more of a gift of awareness rather than a curse of moodiness. It's all about how you can channel your sensitivities toward empowerment. I personally often find that in the days prior to my bleed my dream state is heightened and intuitive, and energetic downloads from spirit are increased.

During your time in autumn I suggest that you ask yourself the following questions:

1. What have I been avoiding or neglecting in my life?
2. Where can I say no instead of yes?
3. What is no longer working in my life and needs to change?
4. Am I being kind to myself or am I being overly self-critical?

Affirmation for autumn:
"I use my heightened sensitivities to bring to light my inner truth."

When you begin to start tracking your menstrual cycle with a focus on other aspects of the inner discoveries your bleed may bring you, as opposed to simply *when it's due* it brings a whole new dimension to the world of menstruation.

You begin to understand that a woman's bleed runs much deeper than simply one week a month, it's a tapestry and intrinsic weaving of all the inner seasons to make a whole. As you further discover your personal connection to your inner seasons it enables you to deepen your awareness to your needs as a woman and accommodate these throughout the month for a life that flows more easily and with greater productivity. You begin to see how you may capitalise on events throughout the month and where possible schedule these in alignment with your own personal rhythm by using your menstrual cycle awareness.

Naturally you may not be able to accommodate every aspect of your monthly *to do list* alongside that of your cycle but once you have started to become more in tune with your body and how you feel as each week progresses through cycle awareness where possible, you can arrange your outer world alongside your inner world. This is when using menstrual cycle awareness can be your ultimate tool for empowerment.

As previously mentioned, during your inner winter phase you are more inclined to want to retreat and be more solo in nature. Therefore, why not schedule a date in your diary to do just that—retreat, make a date with yourself. Whether it's blocking off an hour, half a day or whatever you can accommodate, bringing self-care into your life at this particular time in your cycle is crucial. Trust me, you will notice the following month where you have truly listened to your body, nurtured your body and closely paid attention. Your cycle awareness catches up with you and it's usually in the month that follows that you can see how much or how little self-care was attended to in the month prior.

New ideas tend to emerge during the time of your inner spring after the shedding of the week prior in your bleed. This is a great time to undertake tasks that require inspiration, enthusiasm and a sense of using your creative abilities to their full potential. Undertaking tasks that require your full focused attention are opportunistic here in this phase.

If you have a social event to host, using time during your inner summer is a perfect way of harnessing the power of your social butterfly instincts and being happy about being the centre of attention.

Menstrual cycle awareness brings rise to the importance of a woman filling her own cup. We simply cannot go on from month to month and then in turn, year to year depleting ourselves and expecting that the body will not suffer in some form. When we honour our cycle and give yourself as a woman the nurturing support we so often give out to others you can begin to come back home to yourself and the full expression of all you can be. An endless summer doesn't serve anybody, we need to bring awareness to all the inner seasons and allow them to work in harmony with one another.

If you have the flexibility within your monthly schedule to prioritise tasks according to your personal cycle you may find that it allows you to maximise life and your full potential as a woman.

So, in a nutshell, you can summarise your cycle in the following manner:

Inner winter: clear your calendar and make a date with yourself, access gentle movement like walking or yoga and slow down and rest where ever possible.

Motto: "Rest is best"

Inner spring: be more of a risk taker during this phase, problem solving and creating projects is heightened, schedule time to socialise with friends, speak up at meetings and go out and tap into your adventurous side, undertaking exercise you love.

Motto: "Master of creativity"

Inner summer: your thoughts and feelings may be easier to verbalise to others and your sex drive may be at its peak as your energy levels tend to be at their highest. Enjoy all forms of exercise where you can.

Motto: "C is for communication"

Inner autumn: this is the time to get on with your *to do lists* as you begin the nesting phase of the month. It's a great time to undertake clutter clearing of all that you do not use or love (chapter 13 explores the art of clutter clearing further).

Autumn is also a great time to increase your self-care with stress reducing activities like massage and undertaking restorative exercise. This is also a great time to start going to bed a little earlier of an evening, particularly in the second half of this week.

Motto: "Get things done"

What you will need in order to track your cycle:

You can obtain a journal that you will dedicate solely to your monthly bleed. Within this journal you can note your feelings, energy levels, appetite and dietary needs, the flow of your bleed (heavy or light), the duration of your bleed, the colour and consistency and your sex drive.

By using a dedicated journal for your cycle awareness, you really have deep insight with following typical trends that occur for yourself and then be able to personalise this for the months that follow.

There are also many Apps available these days on your Smart Phone to help you track your menstrual cycle.

Aromatherapy Connection

The use of essential oils throughout the monthly cycle of a woman can be used to your advantage according to your sensitivities and your needs.

Inner winter: calming oils such as lavender are wonderful to use in this phase. Lavender essential oil allows you to find the stillness, calmness and tranquillity within. During the winter phase of your cycle it is essential that you gift down-time to yourself to rest. The qualities of lavender may enhance your spiritual awareness which is wonderful during this part of your cycle when intuition may be heightened.

Inner spring: citrus oils such as lemon are perfect to compliment this phase. Using lemon essential oil is a wonderful way in which to slowly transition back into the world after your bleed. With its fresh scent and vitality, it helps to fill your life with light again after having been cocooned within. It also brings out your personal zest for life with a youthful energetic spirit.

Inner summer: florals such as rose are beautiful to incorporate in this phase. Rose is often referred to as the *Queen of the flowers*. When you think of how a rose starts off as a tiny bud and then blooms into fullness, this is how you are as a woman during your summer season. Allow rose essential oil to raise your vibration and to feel the fullness of all you can be in this world.

Inner autumn: juniper berry is a wonderful oil to connect with during this phase. It is particularly useful as you embark upon *the void* just prior to your bleed. As the inner critic comes out this oil is wonderful in allowing you to face your fears while being comfortable in your own skin. This oil is most potent during the dark and new moon phase of the lunar cycle or your personal menstrual cycle, helping you to use your magnetic powers of looking into the abyss with the inner knowing that anything is truly possible.

Crystal Connection

Inner winter: moonstone is a great stone to have on your bedside table during your bleed to bring a sense of calm.

Inner spring: selenite allows you the courage to move forward in life.

Inner summer: rose quartz the ultimate stone for self-love.

Inner autumn: citrine to balance hormones and alleviate fatigue.

Place a tumbled stone such as the ones suggested above into a glass of water for a few hours (apart from selenite which is water soluble and therefore cannot be immersed in water) in either sunlight or moonlight and use throughout the particular season. You may use this water over your body e.g. in a bath, placing droplets of water over your body.

Goddess Connection

Call upon the following Goddess energies during the personal phase of your cycle or during the natural season in nature to assist you on your path.

Spring: Branwen – Welsh Goddess of beauty and love. A maiden Goddess of sovereignty and inspiration. She is thought to be Venus, the morning star.

Summer: Aphrodite – Greek Goddess of love and beauty. She allows you to see and know the fullness of your womanly worth.

Autumn: Kali Ma – Hindu Goddess of time. She eradicates and destroys all that is no longer needed, creating space in which all things are possible. During the *void* (the space just prior to your bleed) within the menstrual cycle it gives you the opportunity to bring awareness to what is ready to be let go of during your bleed time.

Winter: Cailleach – Hag Goddess of Scotland. She carries a staff that freezes the ground during the winter months. She is the bringer of death (in the sense of completion of a cycle) and is often depicted looking as such. During the winter phase of your bleed it gifts an opportunity to undertake your own subtle death as you shed the old and prepare for the newness of spring to follow.

Affirmation

"I honour my cycle in all phases of womanhood."

Seed #2

Bring awareness to the changes taking place within your body both physiologically as well as emotionally on a weekly basis. By slowing down and being the sacred observer, you gain a greater awareness toward your menstrual cycle as a whole.

Your connection to your womb throughout all phases of womanhood is your key to being able to witness the power of creativity throughout the month and the healing that occurs as you transition from week to week. Your menstrual cycle awareness is a gift toward a life of balance, joy and productivity throughout all phases of your life, not only during your bleeding years.

CHAPTER 3

By the Light of the Moon

I will never forget the night sky in California at Denise Linn's Star Mountain Ranch. Something is mesmerising about looking up at the vast array of stars in the night sky and capturing a glimpse of Grandmother Moon, no matter what phase she may be in. It's the feeling of connection to the big wide world, the universe around us and how interconnected we are to one another. It's also the concept that everything on our planet and beyond is alive.

It happened to be a full moon on my stay at Star Mountain Ranch during the *Flower Moon*. The flower moon is the first full moon in May, receiving its name from the bounty of flowers that bloom in May. There are 13 full moons within a lunar year. Each moon receives a name in connection to the current natural cycle. Ancient cultures worldwide reflect these moon names as a reflection of the seasonal occurrences in nature.

In North America, during May, colours are abundant within the lush green land as summer approaches. This is in direct contrast to my seasonal weather and cycle back home in Australia, where during this time we are instead preparing for winter.

At Star Mountain Ranch, as a group we held a full moon ceremony. I recall drumming to Grandmother Moon and feeling her essence beaming down upon me as if she were filling me with light within every inch of my being. In ancient times the full moon was when a woman was most fertile, and in many ways the full moon brings out the feeling of expansiveness and reaching our full potential. That's precisely how I felt amongst my sisters under the stars and Grandmother Moon's guidance within our *Red Lotus™ Mystery School* retreat.

In Australia, we are fortunate to have some wonderful wide open spaces to explore under the stars and when a full moon is in the sky, it is extra magical. Many years ago, while spending time in Uluru (Ayers Rock), the stars and the moon glistened above me—an etched memory in my mind. Whilst staying at Star Mountain Ranch during the full moon, this memory came flooding back as I stood underneath the starlit sky. There is magic to be found among the moon and the stars all over our globe. This helps us see how expansive our universe is and how expansive we may be with our hopes, dreams and goals for our future.

In no small way was it a coincidence that I was to attend this retreat during the full moon; travelling solo across the other side of the world was a courageous effort on my part. Leaving my husband and young daughter home in Australia certainly pulled at my heartstrings. There are times in life to pull back, and there are times when it's necessary to feel the fear and do it anyway, and this was one of those times for me. I wasn't entirely sure why it was that I felt the deep desire to pack my bags and travel across the globe, but what I am confident of now is that my soul was calling me forward for the work that I do today and the further work that I am to do tomorrow, assisting women like you, to rise beyond their greatest expectation living life on your terms. So, when you feel the tug, the strong pull toward your destiny, this is your intuition speaking. When you choose to listen and follow that inner guidance, you can be rest assured that there is a bigger purpose and reason than you may ever be aware of at the time. Allow your intuition to be your guide and lean in to follow your heart, and life will open doorways for you like you could never imagine possible. When you are aligned and living your truth, your heart and soul shine and sing for all to see.

As women we have multiple ways in which we may keep in sync with Grandmother Moon's phases and capitalise on her energy. Following the guidance of the moon by acknowledging her phases is a great way to keep with the rhythm and cycle of nature and your natural internal rhythms as a woman. By keeping in sync with the moon phases, we can harness the power of what each aspect of the moon gifts us. Aligning with the cycles and our own rhythms, we instinctively know when to speed up and fill our daily schedule and know that our commitments can be achieved without burnout. We then also know when to slow down and seek rest and renewal to power our body's storehouse.

- We may use our own unique internal moon phase according to our bleed.
- We may use Grandmother Moon as our guiding light if we no longer bleed.
- We may use a combination of both if we are still bleeding to weave her magic into our daily lives.

Great power comes from both our menstrual cycle and lunar wisdom; connecting the two creates a potency of immense magic. As women, we can weave this knowledge to enhance our rhythmic womanly existence and use the energy of the moon for intention setting, manifesting and releasing what no longer serves us, ready to welcome in fresh new energy and vitality in the months ahead.

Most of us are aware and various research supports that the moon profoundly affects our psyche. When we look back into ancient times and the times of our ancestors, we were so much more aligned with nature and our natural rhythms. Women would menstruate together under a new moon and ovulate under a full moon. In times gone by, women would also set aside ancient rituals of gathering at this powerful moon time. Today we tend to spend so much time inside under artificial lighting and other mitigating factors that our natural biological rhythms may differ from that of our ancestors. There is now a resurgence of some of our ancient ways and a desire to reconnect to our natural rhythm and flow of life as a woman.

This is an area I love to help guide and coach women with. There always appears to be an air of magic that surrounds us when gathering within the circles I facilitate to celebrate the new moon or full moon. This is the same the world over when women gather to share in sacred rituals and ceremony honouring the current phase of the moon. You can always feel a sense of expansion within a room full of women honouring their connection to Grandmother Moon and the monthly gifts she shares. Allow yourself to become more curious by connecting to the moon phases and seeking out a women's circle online or within your hometown to help lift and elevate you further on your pathway to the Goddess within.

The moon goes through cycles much like we do through birth, growth, full bloom, harvest, decay, death and then back to rebirth. Grandmother Moon is our cosmic guide, and you may be feeling the pull to dive deep and discover your connection. In the following pages I will share with you how to deepen your connection and the understanding of how the moon is broken up into eight moon phases and what these mean regarding capitalising on her wisdom.

I like to think of the moon as a rose starting as a tight bud at the new moon and then blossoming to become gloriously in full bloom at the time of the full moon. Generally, most of us take more notice of the full moon when it's luminous, bright and all the hype that goes with it—legends of werewolves, higher crime rates and emergency department admissions etc or for rituals and releasing what no longer serves us. We then tend to look to the new moon as another notable phase where new beginnings occur and planting seeds in the fertile soil of our soul. But there are six other phases of the moon that hold importance too but are less publicised and generally get less attention. The more in tune you can become with all phases of the moon, the more in tune you become with your life and how to use these phases to your advantage.

Let's start at the beginning in the dark phase of the moon and work toward full bloom under the illuminating guidance of the full moon.

New Moon

This is where we plant the seeds to birth our magnificent futures with a clean slate, so imagine the sight of a tight rosebud just starting out. This is the time when we are full of hope and potential, and our dreams are brewing inside of us. This is an intensely magical time for manifestation.

This is also the phase linked to the time of menstruation. In ancient times, women tended to receive their bleed together under this phase. The new moon is a time of heightened intuition and inner awareness. A time to retreat, to go within and build our inner strength through rest and renewal. For women, it's often a time when we perhaps do not wish to be in big crowds and be the centre of attention; it can often be that we feel drawn to a more quiet and reflective time in our month where we want to be the silent observer and sit back and watch the world go by—taking time to curl up on the sofa with a good book and a warm cup of tea or coffee, or to spend more time resting. In a world that is often so fast-paced, the time of the new moon is a perfect opportunity to permit ourselves to slow down.

Our senses are often heightened at this time, and our psychic abilities are enhanced. This makes way to further step up your devotional practice with more profound meditation, prayer, manifesting, and sharing your wisdom with your fellow sisters.

Waxing Crescent Moon

This is the time when the rosebud is just starting to slowly open, allowing you to have the courage and faith to begin exploring your ideas and dreams. It gives you a nudge to keep working toward your goals and what you wish to bring forward.

First Quarter Moon

This is the phase one week after the new moon, where we are starting to commit to the goals and visions we planted at the initial new moon phase. This is near the halfway point where the rose is really starting to open up. It's a time to surge forward with our ideas; if we are truly and honestly committed to them and powerfully allow our ideas to take hold and become established.

This is connected to the phase of pre-ovulation when women can often feel like they can do a million things at once and still have the energy to do more! We are ready, willing and able to step out into the world and give it our all.

This phase of Grandmother Moon is the time to take risks, to *feel the fear and do it anyway* type of attitude. Women can often feel more social and have more energy to exercise. This phase is an opportune time to launch new projects and ideas into the world.

Gibbous Moon

This is where the moon is coming to a peak; the rose is really starting to blossom now and soulfully bloom and in doing so our ego is starting to truly work over time. This can also be the time when you are tested in strength and endurance to keep going but it's also a great time to review your original plans and modify them if you need to.

Full Moon

This is where Grandmother Moon reaches her peak, it's make-or-break time! The rose has bloomed, fully open in its beautiful splendour and glory. Things come to a head at this time and it's literally make or release time; everything is being revealed. It's when emotions bubble and rise to the surface and our ideas and full expression are out in the world. It's also a great time for gratitude and forgiveness.

As a woman, this is when we are most fertile and the time of ovulation. It's when we have more energy to use and want to be seen and heard more in the world. We are in our most voluptuous and sensual phase and we don't mind who sees! All eyes can be on us, and it's often the time we relish this attention.

Disseminating Moon

This is where the actualisation of our ideas comes in, and it is often where we can take a sigh of relief and let go. This is like when you've organised something massive, you've planned for weeks, and then the big event happens and it's over; you flop and take in that big breath and sigh before re-grouping again. This is the perfect time to rest and re-gather your internal forces.

Third Quarter Moon

This phase of the moon gives you a chance to go back and review the past weeks and see what's worked and what hasn't. The rose that was in full bloom is also starting to shed and those petals are gently falling to the earth. You are beginning to make room for new energy to come in again.

This is the time post-ovulation when our energy levels start to decrease and we may wish to start retreating from the world around us, wanting more alone time. This is when you need to focus on preserving your energy by trying to catch earlier bedtime routines or to journal more and prepare to go inward.

Balsamic Moon

This is the last part of the lunar cycle, surrendering to spirit within and allowing the final petals of your rose to drop away. It's a time that our lessons and all the wise knowledge of the entire cycle is revealed. We move into acceptance and healing mode and move into the way of dream weaving again as we head toward another new moon phase.

When you can follow the phases of the moon and how you feel during the lunar month, particularly when you can bring that awareness into your life on a regular lunar basis, you can anchor yourself into the ritual of intention and manifestation.

Our ancestors had calendars based around the moon. We can also use this age-old ancient practice to enhance our lives today in modern times. Following the phases of the moon and our personal moons enables us to keep showing up as our most empowered selves.

While there are eight phases of the moon, many like to focus on the four main concepts that are divided into:

New Moon: set your intentions.

Waxing Moon: work toward bringing your intentions to physical form.

Full Moon: completion and reflection on what is no longer working.

Waning Moon: time to release and let go and change direction in life where required.

You may also like to notice what each sign of the zodiac gifts you during a particular moon phase as you deepen your awareness of the rhythms and cycles of nature as a means to live an even more fulfilling life.

Whether you live in the southern hemisphere like I do, or you are a northern hemisphere sister, we all see the same moon phase on the same date. A new moon is represented by the zodiac sign we are currently in while the opposing sun sign represents a full moon. Aries is always considered to be the commencement of the zodiac and astrological new year.

Aries 21 March-19 April
New Moon in Aries has a Full Moon in Libra

Taurus 20 April-20 May
New Moon in Taurus has a Full Moon in Scorpio

Gemini 21 May-20 June
New Moon in Gemini has a Full Moon in Sagittarius

Cancer 21 June-22 July
New Moon in Cancer has a Full Moon in Capricorn

Leo 23 July-22 August
New Moon in Leo has a Full Moon in Aquarius

Virgo 23 August-22 September
New Moon in Virgo has a Full Moon in Pisces

Libra 23 September-22 October
New Moon in Libra has a Full Moon in Aries

Scorpio 23 October-21 November
New Moon in Scorpio has Full Moon in Taurus

Sagittarius 22 November-21 December
New Moon in Sagittarius has a Full Moon in Gemini

Capricorn 22 December-19 January
New Moon in Capricorn has a Full Moon in Cancer

Aquarius 20 January-18 February
New Moon in Aquarius has a Full Moon in Leo

Pisces 19 February-20 March
New Moon in Pisces has a Full Moon in Virgo

Astrology and understanding the zodiac is a fascinating area of study and may help enhance your connection to the phases of the sun and moon in your life. For more information, you can divulge a little further and investigate the qualities and attributes that each zodiac season holds. If you are new to astrology in general, a great way to start is by looking at your own sun sign according to your birth date. This, in turn directly impacts your womanly insights and wisdom to express out into the world.

Aromatherapy Connection

Use the following essential oils in an oil diffuser or vaporiser throughout the following phases of the moon or the particular phase of your monthly cycle to enhance your vitality throughout the month.

New Moon: Patchouli

This essential oil has an extremely rich, sweet herbaceous, spicy and woody odour. It can help to start afresh by having a harmonising and stabilising effect on the mind, especially when overthinking things in life. It lets you get back in touch with your body and sensuality.

Waxing Moon: Juniper Berry

This essential oil has a fresh, woody-sweet and pine-needle-like odour. It is a beautiful oil to aid in regeneration with its fresh, clean scent associated with the purification of body, mind and spirit.

Full Moon: Ylang Ylang

This essential oil has a powerful floral, almost seductive and intensely sweet odour with a woody undertone. It is known to have a calming effect, reducing stress and is even classified as an aphrodisiac. This oil creates a feeling of peace and as a woman, can help to bring out your feminine side more and radiate more confidence.

Waning Moon: Geranium

This essential oil has a distinct leafy-rosy scent (often reminds me of an English country garden). This oil can be described as having mother-like qualities creating a sense of security and stability and encouraging you to use your imagination and intuition more.

Using the above oils throughout the moon's phases really allows you to tune into the messages you receive and feel within your body.

Crystal Connection

As an avid lover of the crystal kingdom, I have crystals all over my home and workplace to assist me throughout my life. Not only do they look amazing, but their energy elevates their space.

When it comes to the moon, there are a couple of crystals that are my ultimate loves:

- Moonstone
- Selenite

Moonstone is a wonderful crystal to use to assist with the lunar energy. It is closely related to the female cycle and is said to assist with menstrual cramps and also help during pregnancy. While travelling throughout India I collected some unique pieces of moonstone. In India, they often refer to moonstone as *dream stones* assisting with visions during our dream state.

Selenite is closely related to Goddess Selene, the moon Goddess; this is one of my most favourite crystals. I have a piece of selenite on my bedside table and always have a piece in my luggage ready for my accommodation when travelling (along with numerous others, not to mention adding to my collection throughout my global travels).

Regarding ritual and ceremony, the most crucial aspect you must consider is your intention, as the intention is everything! Working with crystals, particularly when honouring the moon phase, is a powerful tool for healing. One time during a women's circle I was facilitating around the lead-up toward a full moon, we worked with selenite in ritual and ceremony with powerful results. We were celebrating around the full moon in Aries for this particular gathering, and as the energies of the moon were called forth together with Goddess Selene, you could feel the vibration of the room shift and elevate. We utilised a selenite dagger in this ceremony to undertake a transformative cord-cutting and releasing exercise. The act of forgiveness upon a full moon is mighty powerful and this combined with the use of selenite, created a container for an abundance of healing to take place.

When working with crystals, it is always recommended to allow them to bathe under the moonlight from time to time to charge (weather dependent as certain crystals are sensitive to water—selenite is one of these crystals). Of course, there are many other means to charge crystals. Still, moonlight, particularly the full moon, is often a ritual many crystal lovers embrace with powerful results.

Goddess Connection

Goddess Selene, the Greek Goddess of the moon, can assist you in your dream time throughout your night's rest. She is usually shown riding a horse or chariot with a crescent moon for her crown. As previously mentioned, when working with the crystal kingdom, selenite is a beautiful stone to connect with the moon's energies.

Set an intention to connect with Goddess Selene upon retreating at the end of a long day, allowing her wisdom to flow into your dreams in the following manner:

Still your mind and centre yourself as you lay in bed, ready for a restful night's sleep and inwardly state:

"Dear Goddess Selene, I ask that you please be with me during my dream state, allowing your wisdom to flow to me and through me. I also ask that upon waking, I recall this wisdom for the highest good of all. Thank you."

It has been said that Selene would drive over the night sky in her chariot, gifting the sky its light. You can conjure this image in your mind's eye as you recite the above prayer.

Artemis and Hecate are other Goddesses of the moon that you may consider working with also.

Soulful Exercise

Start to get curious about how you wish your life to feel in the coming time; use your imagination here and dream big. When we start focusing on the moon and using her energies as a way of planting seeds in the fertile soil of our soul, bringing action toward making these manifestations take physical form, releasing what isn't working and altering our path where needed, we create our reality.

One way to further assist you along this path is by creating a vision board. I have seen time and time again how these creations can bring to life all that we wish to manifest. Collect pictures from magazines, postcards, images, and words of how you would like to feel when your dreams, hopes, wishes and desires for the future come to fruition. Consider cutting out these images and then pasting them onto cardboard (some people these days even do them in an online format, so do what works best for you). These soulful creations act as a way to help keep you on track as each moon passes and you focus on and re-evaluate your goals.

Another way of looking at your vision board is to create a board that reflects the woman you want to bring to light even further in the time to come. Who is she? What does she need to do to bring her out of the shadows? How does this gorgeous Goddess within feel when she has all that she desires? Allow your creative juices to flow during this exercise, have fun and allow yourself to dream your world into being.

Creating my own Goddess vision board has been one of the many ways I have magnetised my future, helping to bring out my inner Goddess further. I often place my vision boards upon my home meditation altar so that it is in regular view, and I can ask myself questions from time to time about what the images mean and any feelings evoked.

Affirmation

The power of affirmations during the eight phases of the moon can be an excellent way for you to connect to their strength and what each phase can gift you throughout the month.

New Moon: *"I reclaim my womanly essence and embrace new beginnings"*.

Waxing Crescent Moon: *"I create an action plan for my future"*.

First Quarter Moon: *"I easily and effortlessly flow toward my goals"*.

Waxing Gibbous Moon: *"I sit in my power and in harmony with all that surrounds me"*.

Full Moon: *"I am ready to embrace all of me and shine my light into the world"*.

Waning Gibbous Moon: *"I love and celebrate all of my accomplishments"*.

Third Quarter Moon: "*As each day passes, I gather in strength and wisdom*".

Waning Crescent Moon: "*As I surrender and let go, I receive opportunities for growth*".

Seed #3

Harness the power of the current phase of the moon cycle (together with your personal bleed time if this is still occurring) to understand the wisdom that each cycle is sharing with you. There is magic in the lunar phases; look up and feel Grandmother Moon's love fill your womanly essence and the sacred container of your womb.

When you allow yourself to connect to Grandmother Moon's phases, rhythms and cycles, your life as a wise woman expands mentally, emotionally, spiritually and physically.

CHAPTER 4

The Gift of Menopause

The road has been long, arduous, and filled with many twists and turns. Career changes, relationship hurdles, grief and pain, love and excitement have occurred. The constant ebbing and flowing within life's journey is being met with courage and an understanding of a larger mission at play. On graduation day, I sit back in awe of all I have endured, and with a confident smile on my face, I can say, "You made it… and the best is yet to come."

This is how I view my time reaching menopause (at present, I am still receiving my bleed each month, in the phase of motherhood). I am truly excited to exercise my crone wisdom when the time comes for me to graduate. I like viewing menopause as a form of *graduation*, having successfully passed through the ranks of *maiden, mother, maga* and finally reaching the *crone* years.

The rites of passage through womanhood are discussed within this chapter, being that of maiden (birth and beginnings of menstruation and becoming a woman), mother (childbirth or the birthing of a creative endeavour), maga (early years of menopause and toward retirement), crone (the late stages of our lives and living out the truth of our wisdom).

As mentioned, I am currently living through the phase of late motherhood, yet to experience all the facets of menopause (although in recent times I have been experiencing hot flushes with sudden bursts of heat, particularly in my chest, neck and face). What I do have on my side though, is a deep understanding of the critical lessons that play out each month of my bleed (having spent over a decade of actively utilising menstrual cycle awareness) in preparation for this graduation day; this is what I am going to share with you in this chapter.

In this space, we honour all phases and stages of life as a woman, and help those who, like me, still bleed to receive the most out of their monthly gift. On average a woman may receive approximately four hundred and fifty menstrual bleeds in her lifetime. In conjunction with those women who still receive their bleed, in this space is an opportunity to continue to also honour and support those further down the road of womanhood who may not have had the awareness or opportunity to encapsulate the wisdom of their bleeding years.

Every stage along the womanhood journey is vital. Within each phase, we experience life cycle aspects from birth, childhood, adolescence, adulthood, and becoming an elder. Similarly, we go through aspects of birth, decay, death and rebirth. This is what unites all the phases we are on as a woman; we may be on a different path, but ultimately, we are all on the same journey toward the graduation of our crone years after menopause.

As women, we all have gifts to share. This is why the bonds between maiden, mother, maga and crone must be united. We learn, grow and evolve at different speeds, and yet each aspect of womanhood holds its own potent wisdom. Exercising deep respect for one another is how we assist each other along the pathway, so that at the end of our days as a wise old crone, we know wholeheartedly that we gave life our all.

Imagine a stunning red rose, the rose is beautiful as a tiny bud, just as it is beautiful in full bloom. When the rose petals fall upon the earth, it is no less beautiful than when on the bush, yet it takes on a new level of beauty scattered upon the ground, ready to be used in a new way in nature, and then a new cycle follows. The evolution of the rose can be likened to the way we as women evolve throughout our rites of passage into menopause and beyond.

How we view our first bleed in menarche often sets a seed within us as a woman for our entire menstruating years. Therefore, if by the time we come to menopause, we have had a less than positive experience throughout our bleeding years, it can significantly impact how our menopausal life plays out. We may view menopause negatively, seeing it fearfully as another obstacle of physical changes to endure and a burden of stress to overcome.

Equally said, if our years of bleeding have been more manageable and cycle awareness has taken shape to allow us to see the wisdom within the monthly cycle, it also greatly impacts our menopausal life. We can view the changes ahead in our lifestyle as a time of great reflection and inspiration toward the new beginning of the next phase of our rich and full life.

From over two decades of coaching and healing, I have often found that the way your potential future path into menopause plays out is significantly aligned with the way you respond and view your bleed as a whole. I have discovered that more and more women are seeking to understand further what takes place within their bodies on a spiritual level—not just the physical, during the monthly cycle as a woman.

In recent years, the state of one's mental health is being addressed more than it ever has previously. To assist our mental health, we as a society are looking toward spiritual avenues such as meditation, yoga, and relaxation to calm the mind, bringing conscious awareness to the body, while also regulating the nervous system back to a state of balance. This, in turn, assists the physical self; bringing menstrual cycle awareness and the menopause journey into focus is yet another link in the chain toward understanding the female body more intimately.

Throughout my coaching and healing, I have also worked alongside women of various phases of womanhood, and I recognise that each individual has a unique connection to their power as a woman. Some are aware of this power and use it to enhance their lifestyle, while other women have their power hidden, and some are starting to awaken.

My client, Rachael, works within the corporate world and is in a position where she often needs to lead training for her team and presentations to board members. Wherever it is possible, she likes to coordinate these meetings during the follicular phase of her menstrual cycle (approximately days 6-12), when she feels the most confident and her energy is more vibrant. Naturally, meetings can't always be scheduled during these times. Still, she knows within herself this phase is where she feels she can take charge and *go for it*, leading with strength and conviction.

At the other end of the spectrum, I have another client, Jennifer, who is retired and post-menopausal. She is now using the power of her womb space to awaken creative projects within her that she has never felt she had the time for previously. She is now devoting more time to work on herself and putting herself at the centre of her universe. This is in contrast to how life has been in previous phases of womanhood, where she was nurturing the needs of others. She is now tracking her cycle through the phase of the moon (the new moon acts like the time of your bleed after menopause) to help use her inner power to its full advantage. As you recall, in chapter 3, we discussed the potency of working with the moon's phases to assist our positive lifestyle choices.

As women, we all have access to this personal power; we hold the key to our wisdom and as we each step into our light, we are starting to desire the use of this key even more.

As I have previously mentioned, there are always dualities—light and shadow. We can never have one without the other; both are necessary for us to grow and evolve. When a woman thinks about menopause, she can often go straight to the negatives—mood swings, hot flushes, weight change, etc. Women do not always see the beauty or spiritual empowerment side of menopause. I believe this is a crucial component that can profoundly impact how we view our experience as modern women.

Becoming more aware of the special significance that menopause can bring to you as a woman will help shift your thinking into a more positive frame. In turn, the changes within the female body and the life of the woman living through it can be seen through the eyes of excitement, enthusiasm and vibrancy.

Menopause has many beautiful aspects that help a woman view her worth in a different light; it awakens the wise woman within. A new sense of independence and a deeper awareness of inner identity emerges.

The woman who understands herself is no longer willing to stand back and have someone else tell her who *she* should be. When a woman comes into her power (owning all of who she is), she is making a bold, courageous statement to the world that she is ready to stand up, be heard, and lead the life she was brought here to do in such a way that evokes sheer excitement. This excitement, this glow, this inner radiance, can be felt not only in herself but by those around her; it's captivating, mesmerising, and magnetic. It is a sweeping wand of empowered light. This light is not coming from ego but from the inner spark of creativity that lies within her womb space.

There is a Native American proverb that states that during menarche (the onset of a young maiden's first bleed), she discovers her power. During her menstruating years, she practices her power. Then at menopause, she becomes her power. I exquisitely love this as it perfectly demonstrates how transformational this time in a woman's life can be. A far cry from all the physical trials and tribulations, it's a time to be embraced and lovingly see yourself blossoming and blooming into a version of yourself that is more aligned with your purpose and what is most meaningful to you in life.

There is no denying that the menopause phase will have some ups and downs. Know these times of transition are not forever. Along the way though, menopause brings you opportunities to discover more personal growth. Riding the waves of emotion and physical changes throughout this phase is a powerful way of bringing you closer to who you truly are at your core. As women, we all eventually go through this time of transition, breathing a deep exhalation, knowing that eventually we all reach the other side!

In many ways, each month throughout your bleeding years, you are given an opportunity to see little glimpses into what going through menopause is like. The build-up just before your bleed is much likened to the early stages of menopause. Once the bleed has finished, it's like an act of liberation, a wild and free aspect where you shine entirely from the inside out. You can achieve anything. The phases of our menstruating years, from the luteal phase, to ovulation, to the follicular phase, and then finally through to menstruation create a comparison to how the menopause process can feel for a woman, albeit through a different lens.

Phases of menstruation:
- The luteal phase refers to the time between ovulation and before receiving your menstrual bleed.
- Ovulation refers to the release of the egg from the ovary.
- The follicular phase refers to the time between the first day of your period (when you commence bleeding) to ovulation.
- Menstruation is the shedding of the uterine lining with old blood and tissue.

Seeing menopause through spiritual eyes as an awakening to shine your light brighter in this world is truly a gift. It brings a sense of freedom to accept the past and focus our attention on the future and how we want to step out and be seen in the world. It is a gift often not opened by many women in our modern world today. In times gone by, rites of passage were seen as significant in allowing us to acknowledge the changes in our bodies, not just physically, but on an emotional, mental and spiritual level.

How you experienced your first bleed as a young maiden impacts your menstruating years as a mother. By *mother*, remember that I am referring to the triple Goddess aspect of maiden, mother, crone regarding the phases you go through on your path toward menopause and becoming wholeheartedly the woman you were born to be.

In the past, we had rites of passage that were honoured and celebrated within communities, such as the rite of birth, rite of adolescence, rite of menarche, rite of marriage, rite of parenthood, rite of eldership etc. These rites of passage in times gone by were crucial in allowing us to own our power throughout each phase. These days, our significant rites of passage are downplayed, dismissed, or never even given a second thought.

Therefore, by the time menopause comes along, for many women, it's seen as a burden—another aspect of life as a woman that is met with a sigh and grunt of disgust. Instead of seeing it as an opportunity to honour the passage of time travelled from being that young maiden, watching herself grow into a woman, perhaps birthing children if that is her path, or possibly birthing a business, a career, a creative endeavour, and then finally arriving at this significant turning point where life opens up possibilities and ignites creative sparks like never before.

The rite of marriage is so readily accepted within our modern society. Parties and celebrations go along with this milestone. There is such excitement toward this time and the build-up that goes along with it (whether for the bridal couple themselves or those witnessing the celebration between two people within their community). The same can be said when a child graduates high school.

With any transition in life, there is always potential for grief and sadness. Menopause can create a sense of grieving the loss of youth. Once a woman can get over the initial hurdle of the sense of *loss* as the world as she knows it crumbles, it eventually gives rise to a new way of viewing life with hope, excitement, and more profound love and acceptance of self.

There are many steps to help you along the menopause journey, and I am passionate about helping women like you consciously walk the path toward menopause enlightenment and your empowered self.

Let us change how we see menopause from here on out, and allow the rite of menopause to be seen as an invitation to bring present consciousness into yet another fantastic milestone of life. One that is deserving of its own celebration.

The following are some examples of how you can cope with the changes during menopause:

- Ensure that you are eating healthily and drinking adequate amounts of water.
- Ensure that you rest regularly, particularly as your sleep patterns at night may be disturbed and irregular.
- Exercising regularly is a great way to keep stress levels down and boost your mood.
- Participating in activities like yoga, meditation, and breathwork are powerful ways to keep you grounded and foster a positive mindset toward everything changing within you.
- Stay connected to friends (particularly girlfriends who may be going through the phase along with you) and family. It is imperative that you keep the lines of communication open.
- Stay focused on all the wonderful things you are good at and celebrate all the things you love about yourself.

Looking at menopause through kind, loving eyes and an air of excitement for all the new opportunities ahead is a positive way of looking at this transitional phase, allowing you to see how magnificent you are and always have been. A woman who is now ready to say, "this is me, and I am so grateful, now let me go out into the world and show just how magnificent I am without apology."

Over the years working alongside women in various stages of womanhood, I have discovered the variance in perspective when it comes to menopause. Some women loathe the thought of *going through the change* and can't wait to be *rid of* their bleeding years. Then other women are content to embrace the world as it comes to them, including the transition into their crone years.

In our modern world, we tend to worship youth and beauty; we only need to pick up a women's magazine to see the images on display showcasing what beauty is. Often, a distorted view of the modern woman is depicted. In contrast, the ageing process is covered up in a struggle toward denying the beauty and inner wisdom that comes with age itself.

The fear of the unknown in life is something we deal with consistently; it never really goes away. However, facing our fears ensures that they do not control us and that we are the ones who steer our own ship. The same can be said regarding our thoughts toward menopause. As a woman grows into her menopausal years, it can often be one of the most frightening and misunderstood aspects of womanhood, with the woman not knowing what to expect. This aspect of womanhood and the time of ageing represents the cycle of destruction and decay and ultimately leads to the end of our days. Therefore, it is no wonder that many in our society today may view it with doom and gloom, but it need not be the case.

When taken with a different perspective and given a positive narrative, the menopausal years are the time of the wise woman or midwives of old. The word crone is derived from the ancient word for crown. When seen like this, it's an honour having received a halo of light for reaching this sacred time. The days of opportunity to bear children are now gone, and a woman's time to step into the wisdom keeper and the healer can come forward. These aspects of the divine feminine are explored further in chapter 13, when we dive more into the mystical powers of living out the way of the Goddess in our everyday life.

In times gone by, this aspect of womanhood was sought after by many as a guide during transitions or when people sought guidance within their kingdom.

If you also think back to the times of the middle ages, these wise women in their crone years were so feared that many were killed during the Inquisition. These women were given names like "witch," or "hag." These images are often summed up in our fairy tales today, depicting these wise women to be seen as someone to fear and a woman's ageing as something to dismiss, wanting to avoid the overall ageing process wherever possible.

Thankfully, the tide is slowly turning, and women are starting to reclaim their power and to see the beauty in every aspect of their sacred womanhood—even more so in their senior years when their inferiority, insecurity and lack of self-worth that was possibly prevalent in their youth (when there has been less life experience and a sense of naivety) disappears in place of strength, courage and wise leadership, having discovered so much about themselves along their path. Crossing the threshold into cronehood is a cause for celebrating the crown you have earned throughout every other rite of passage toward becoming an elder in society.

Reviewing your life from your bleeding years to your current phase of womanhood allows you to see where there is still work to be done while also assisting you in healing the past to fully emerge into the wise woman you were born to be. I have created journal prompts further in this chapter for you to spend time in quiet reflection, taking note of your view and perspective of this phase of womanhood.

The wise woman who has reached her crone years has a depth of life experience, having learned lessons to enable her to fully accept and love herself for who she is and all that she has accomplished with a sense of power that can never be taken from her.

Whatever phase and stage you are in, there is always room to improve and evolve. Your magnificence shines not because of your age, status or external beauty. Your brilliance shines its brightest when you allow yourself to bring ownership to where you are in your life as a woman, whole and complete, just as you are.

This sense of ownership in life as a woman can be depicted through the eyes of a client whom I have worked with for many years toward her womanhood journey. Cindy first started to see me when her daughter, Abby, was younger. Abby has since graduated from University and has recently become engaged. These celebratory aspects are rites of passage on their own. I have witnessed Cindy go through so much change in the cycle of life, letting go of the little girl she gave birth to in order for her daughter to start an independent life of her own. Cindy gave birth to Abby later in life, having had a second marriage, and she started seeing me just before her peri-menopausal years.

I have observed how she endured the rollercoaster of emotions throughout her early menopause with much adulation. Initially, during menopause, she felt a sense of betrayal, particularly as giving birth to Abby was such a memorable experience as she never thought she would have children of her own. To Cindy, the fact that her eggs were no longer viable was seen as a sense of loss. She was grieving the loss of her fertile years as a maiden and mother. It's not that she wanted to have any more children, but more that it was no longer an option, and that part of her life had finished.

She felt like she was becoming old, unattractive, and potentially replaceable, and it was an aspect she wasn't prepared to be feeling. She started to question her attractiveness to her husband. Insecurities began to emerge that he may look elsewhere to a more youthful, effervescent and sensually voluptuous woman as opposed to how she perceived herself to look during ageing.

She had hit a brick wall and so desperately wanted to breathe new life into herself, but all she felt was grief and sadness toward her body that once was supple, firm and sexy and was now visibly showing signs of age and wear and tear.

Over the years and during our time together for healing, I observed her go through these changes. Cindy discovered deep inner healing as she started to honour her time as a woman with more self-care routines, including a regular meditation practice. She gave herself time to breathe and the space to acknowledge that despite her daughter no longer needing her in the same way she used to, she was always going to be her mother. She allowed herself to explore more of the things that brought her joy in life and time with her loving husband undertaking adventures of a new kind, in a new way.

Through menopause, she began to discover herself as the centre of her universe instead of always giving to others first. She learned the art of acceptance and a deeper connection to self-love. It was then that Cindy soon realised that her emergence into menopause enabled her newfound sense of freedom to be herself and give ownership to the life she wanted to create for her crone years to come.

Soulful Exercise

Journalling brings a sense of present-day consciousness and awareness. To review and reflect upon your years so far through womanhood and your perception of the time to come, I have created journal prompts for you to explore. Allow yourself to be free flowing with your writing (don't be concerned with grammar and punctuation, get the words onto the page).

If you have yet to experience an aspect of womanhood, please include how you currently feel toward the thought of this phase.

1. How was your experience of your first bleed?
2. Was there significant female support in your life at this time? How did this impact your experience? If not, what feelings did this evoke within you?
3. If you could speak to your maiden self through this rite of passage today, what words of wisdom would you share with her?

4. How would you describe your bleeding years?
5. How would you encapsulate your view on menstruation?
6. Did bearing children become a part of your rite of passage in womanhood? If so, how do you feel this impacted you in society and as an individual? If you did not bear children, how do you feel this impacted you in society as an individual? What other areas did you create and give birth to throughout your life (e.g. your career)?
7. How would you describe your peri-menopausal years?
8. If you are yet to reach the time of peri-menopause, what are your beliefs of the time to come?
9. When your bleeding years ceased to exist, how did you feel?
10. What were your early thoughts on menopause, and do you still feel the same way today?
11. If you have reached the time of the wise woman (your crone years), are you content with where you are at? If not, how may you alter your lens and perspective to bring further evolution on your path?
12. Summarise your overall experience as a woman with all the lessons you have endured to date; what do your experiences share with you?

Divide up your experience as a woman, using one word how would you describe:
- Your maidenhood (0-25 years)
- Your motherhood (25-50 years)
- Your magahood (50-70 years)
- Your cronehood (70-death)

Are you aware of any areas you wish to explore further regarding your womanhood?

Take time afterwards to review the answers to the questions, paying particular attention to any recurring themes in your thoughts. These questions are a great way to become curious and to highlight areas to continue exploring toward inner healing.

As women, we are all unique. We have all had varying experiences throughout our time on this earth. These lessons of inner growth are ours to experience. Within each experience we may have, there is a hidden power to tap into, which strengthens as time passes. The gift of menopause is to use this power for your highest good.

I will now share specific aspects of aromatherapy that I have found work brilliantly alongside the journey of womanhood.

Aromatherapy Connection

Some essential oils contain phytoestrogens (plant-based compounds which mimic oestrogen in the body), which can help balance hormones and relieve symptoms of menopause. Use these in a diffuser within your home to bring about a sense of balance and comfort.

Some of these essential oils are:
- Clary Sage: this earthy, slightly nutty scent can help bring you back into your body and helps with hot flushes, night sweats and other menopausal symptoms. It enables you to feel the pleasure of the current moment while also acting as a natural anti-depressant.
- Geranium: this floral scent (similar to the smell of roses with a mint-like overtone) is a calming mood lifting oil, wonderful for the heart chakra.
- Jasmine: this exotic floral scent is wonderful to help open your heart, boosting self-confidence and a sense of wellbeing.

- Lavender: this fresh, floral scent (with woody undertones) is beneficial for all the chakras (the energy centres of the body) and is excellent for promoting a sense of calm and can help improve sleep.
- Rose: this sweet, floral scent emanates love and helps to create a soothing atmosphere and assists in calming your emotions.

Use any of the above oils in a diffuser. Add two to three drops of a selected oil mixed with water, which will permeate throughout the home, inducing calming effects. A few drops of essential oil on a handkerchief to carry with you and inhale throughout the day is another way to access the plant kingdom for further healing on your journey of womanhood.

Given the amount of mental fatigue that can occur throughout the menopausal years, it will serve you to set aside time each week for a ritual to unwind, reflect and bring acceptance to where you currently are in your sacred time as a woman.

Running yourself a luxurious bath is a beautiful way to honour the changes taking place within your body, committing to connect to your womb space in a quiet space dedicated to nurturing you and your journey.

When it comes to using essential oils within your bath, it is imperative to understand that they must be mixed with a carrier oil (such as almond or apricot oil), not simply poured into the bathwater, as this may irritate your skin (and sensitive body parts).

I recommend using approximately 3-12 drops of essential oil (of choice) with 1 tablespoon of your desired carrier oil (such as almond or apricot oil) for a single bath. Fill your tub and turn the water off before adding your oil (otherwise, pouring into the hot running water will reduce the oils to merely a beautiful aromatic scent wafting in the room instead of the deeper, therapeutic benefits). Using a carrier oil within the blend will also aid in the skin's hydration and leave your skin with a soft, supple feeling. As you nurture your body, you equally nurture your soul and restore harmony in your life.

Try the following blend to bring about a sense of balance during your bathing ritual.

- 1 tablespoon of desired carrier oil (e.g. almond oil)
- 3 drops of lavender (brings a sense of calm)
- 2 drops of geranium (promotes balance to mind and body)
- 1 drop of ylang ylang (relaxes the mind and feelings of anxiety and overwhelm)

I recommend using this time of self-care to bring more self-awareness into your current feelings and connection to your body and womb. This may be incorporated as a weekly or monthly ritual to honour yourself as the glorious woman you are.

Crystal Connection

I have specifically selected the crystal lepidolite to help you through the menopausal journey. There can often be feelings of grief associated with this powerful time in a woman's life. It's an act of letting go of the woman that was and stepping into the next phase. However, it can be helpful to turn to the crystal kingdom for some added support from Mother Earth during this transition time.

Placing a piece of lepidolite on your bedside table will help bring a sense of calm to the mind ahead of a restful night's sleep. You can also place a piece over your third eye (just between and above your eyebrows) before bedtime as a ten minute wind down and bring a sense of gratitude for the day's events. This ten minute wind down time would also be an excellent opportunity for you to undertake the *Five Gifts of Hathor* gratitude ritual discussed in chapter 1. Lepidolite is often thought of as a peace stone because it has such nurturing and calming properties. These qualities will well serve you throughout all your phases of womanhood, not only in menopause.

Lepidolite connects you to both your third eye (as mentioned) and your sacral chakra (located just below the navel). By connecting to your intuitive side through your third eye and womb space via the sacral chakra, you are allowing an opening to divine wisdom to channel through to you.

Using this crystal in meditation will bring awareness to the wisdom of your crone years while sending healing to the waters of your womb space. It allows you as a woman to transition from the previous ways of being and create a new gateway to step beyond the bleeding years. It also helps to bring more peace and serenity into life, which is often much needed, particularly during this changing phase of womanhood.

Goddess Connection

While there are many Goddess guides that may assist you through the menopausal journey, I would like to introduce you to Hera, the Greek Queen of Heaven. She is the Goddess of the sky, for marriage and women in general. Hera is there to assist you throughout every part of womanhood. Therefore, I feel she is a wonderful Goddess to call upon throughout the sacred rite of passage of menopause. One of her symbols is that of the beautiful peacock. I am fond of the peacock representing the Goddess, particularly as it is also the national symbol for India, and my connections with this land run deep in my veins.

Being the Queen of Mount Olympus, Goddess Hera is a very powerful Goddess. She is also one with both positive and negative attributes (as they all do). She, therefore, helps to sum up the experiences we may go through on the menopausal journey, reflecting upon the past and learning from the errors of our ways in life to turn our wounds into wisdom. She is also noted as a powerful Goddess of marriage and commitment, and marriage in particular, was a sacred act in her eyes. Hera personifies the archetype of a woman who longs all her life to find a marriage partner and feels incomplete without this particular rite of passage. Similar is a woman who is grief-stricken through her desire for children and not having this come to fruition, or equally the birth of a business, only to find it not as successful as one had hoped.

The circumstances surrounding the early years of maiden and mother shape the years of menopause. Coming to terms with your peaks and troughs of life and accepting the past aligns you with your present, enabling your future to be embraced with grace and ease. The Goddess Hera will assist you along this pathway.

Goddess Hera may use her powers to either bless or curse a situation, much like you may do similarly when you view your take on menopause. It is my hope for you that you commence your inner journey to view menopause as a blessing.

Her powers of eternal youth may be called upon in times within your journey when you feel your beauty diminishing and need the reassurance to restore your self-esteem.

Goddess Hera is frequently depicted holding a pomegranate. The pomegranate itself is a symbol of fertility. You may bring Goddess Hera into your everyday world by using such fruit and sprinkling the seeds on a salad. Or fill a bowl with the seeds and place it in your kitchen to remind yourself of the qualities within you as you go about your day.

Bringing the Goddess Hera into your home and making her accessible through sight or taste (such as pomegranate seeds, peacock feathers, white flowers, especially lilies or burning a white candle) helps to remind you of your desire for the need for acceptance along your womanhood journey.

Calling upon Goddess Hera during meditation, particularly when seeking more acceptance of your current experience and phase of womanhood, is highly recommended. Before settling into meditation, evoke her using the following words:

"I now call upon the ancient Goddess Hera and ask that her powers of protection, compassion and motherly instincts assist me in the acceptance of my current experiences through womanhood today."

Be sure to thank her afterwards for her assistance. Note any wisdom received or how you felt during meditation in your journal. Writing down your thoughts and feelings is a powerful way of developing your strength and personal connection to a particular Goddess.

Affirmation

"I embrace and love every aspect of my womanhood; the wise woman within me grows as each day unfolds."

Seed #4

Menopause is one of the greatest gifts of womanhood. The gift of menopause acts as a form of graduation day; you are the scholar and have earned your degree. Celebrate and embrace this time because you have well and truly earned it. Wear your crown with pride and be the beacon for other women as they also aspire to transition through their powerful rites of womanhood.

CHAPTER 5

The Way of the Ancients

Excitement built within me as I gathered around the ancient Drombeg Stone Circle in County Cork, Ireland. The mystical rain fell around me as the mist and fog grew even more dense. The lushness of the green grass and boggy marsh beneath my feet helped to heighten my senses within this land I stood upon. The rolling green hills and trees within the wintery landscape and the distant farm cottages were all food for my soul. The moss covered stones felt magical upon touch, and you could sense the energy emanating from the stone circle. Through my spiritual ears, I could hear the sounds of the *ancients* alongside me as they called me to dance like that of the Druids in times gone by, leaving time and space behind. I was reunited with an ancient hum within my soul that felt the love this land offered me and those who chose to rise to the calling of the earth's energy.

When we allow ourselves to step out of ordinary time, we let a sense of mystery wash over us and allow our intuitive powers as a woman to come alive. This is the magic I find when we create sacred space for ourselves or step into rituals and ceremonies, just like times gone by when people such as the Celts would gather as priestesses and connect through sisterhood power to honour the seasons, to honour the moon, to honour themselves and the expression of life as a woman. As a woman in our modern world, you too may grasp this magic and retrieve this ancient wisdom from the depth of your womb into the realm of current reality.

That cold winter's day among the mystical stones, an umbrella in one hand battling the winds and wild rain, while I mastered the art of jumping puddles in the mud, this stone circle stirred an ancient remembering inside of me. I wanted longingly to evoke more of these feelings for further healing and renewal.

In all of us, there are times when we feel very familiar with our surroundings, a feeling that perhaps we've been there before or that it feels like ancient remembering of times gone by where we have experienced similarities. Ireland is one of those many ancient memories within my soul.

Some of those experiences have been time spent in ritual and ceremony and creating sacred space to go within or feel cocooned within the celebration of life.

In times gone by, women would gather in sacred circles and retreat at the time of their bleed into Moon Lodges or Red Tents.

I love all cultures, and from my experiences across the globe, spending time at sacred sites and relishing in the colour and cultures of various countries brings me immense joy.

As a family, we travelled to Morocco many years ago, and I fell in love with the architecture and overall essence of the land. At my 40th birthday, I wanted to create a Moroccan-themed oasis, and for those who attended my party, it was a celebration like no other! I had fabric draped from the rafters of my home; there were Moroccan lamps, cushions, ottomans, a belly dancer, and Henna tattoos—it had all the feelings of a time in ancient cultural bliss. It was a feeling of being *home* in my soul. It was like an ancient memory of having spent time in these lands in the past and as a woman loving the creative womb-like energy of being in a Red Tent of old.

Different cultures had different names for these sacred places that women would retreat to, but the essence within their philosophy was the same—a returning to the sacred realm of simply being, not doing, whilst at the same time relishing in connection with other women in a community setting.

For the Native Americans, it was affectionately known as the Moon Lodge; in other cultures, it was the Red Tent. The common essence was that it was a place of opportunity for women to heal within the womb-like space amongst their sisters. It was an opportunity to listen to their female elders' stories to share experiences and common union. Often these stories would be repeated time and time again; it's the way it was done in native cultures, allowing these stories to infuse deep within through repetition.

My time spent with my teacher, Denise Linn, at her *Red Lotus Mystery School* in California helped to re-awaken my inner Goddess and an ancient remembering of times gone by when sisters gathering together in sacred rituals and ceremonies was a natural part of life as a woman. There were 13 sisters within our gathering at Star Mountain Ranch (13 representing the number of the Goddess and 13 moons within a lunar year and the concept of 13 menstrual bleeds a year). Denise allowed us to choose our rooms based on a theme. I was naturally drawn to the room called the "Moon Lodge" and instantly felt right at home there.

As previously mentioned, there is the notion that even though in our current life we may not have travelled to faraway lands from where we physically live now, there is an ancient remembering that dwells within our soul of the earth's energy. Denise's idea to commence her *Red Lotus Mystery School* came from a vision of long ago in another life where we all gathered not far from Delphi in Greece, becoming initiates or priestesses of the mystery schools of old (I share more about this in chapter 12). Now, for me personally, in this lifetime, I have never physically travelled to Greece (although it has long been on my wish list! One day, I may get there, but in the meantime, I may harness the power of my meditations, soul journey's and intuitive knowing to travel there). Despite not having been there in this lifetime, when I heard the call to become a part of the *Red Lotus Mystery School* teachings, it felt like I'd come home to my fellow sisters with an ancient remembering deep inside my soul of time spent in these lands (and most likely with the same group of women, albeit in a different lifetime).

Therefore, please allow your intuition and your imagination to flow when thinking about Red Tents or Moon Lodges of old, as there is a deep knowing inside of you that has also experienced this in the past. You would not be drawn to read this book if it were not so. There is a deep longing for all of us as women to return to our roots and the ways of the ancients to bring back this knowledge from yesteryear and weave this into modern times. We can learn much from the past and incorporate these teachings to relate to our current times. So, allow yourself to sink into this concept and see what resonates for you.

The sacred act of entering into a Moon Lodge or Red Tent enables a woman to step out of ordinary time and the everyday activities and busyness of life and enter into the sacred realm of simply *being*. Allowing yourself to dream, rest, and receive spiritual insights and downloads from the Creator, it's also a place to actively practice ritual and ceremony while sending prayers and offerings.

Being able to bring ancient remembering into modern times by honouring our feminine power and the sacredness of the gifts of our moon time is essential.

Where can you create your own inner stillness, especially at your moon time, to retreat, replenish and regenerate? There may be a corner of a room that you can dedicate to the times of the Red Tent and Moon Lodge of old to allow this ancient wisdom to stream forward. Adorn your space with objects that fill you with an essence of the inner Goddess inside of you and your connectedness to Grandmother Moon above and your sisters on this earth plane as well as your galactic star sisters above. Creating an altar within this space may bring a focal point to the energy building each time you frequent this location. Bring aspects of air, water, fire and earth on your altar or aspects of your own connection to the Goddess within. I often also include the plant kingdom through flowers or aromatherapy upon my altars and within my sacred space.

Soulful Exercise

This meditation acts as an initiation rite to help anchor you into the precious nature of your womanhood. So often, our experiences of our first bleed were bypassed and swept over. However, we may trace ourselves back and gift ourselves the opportunity to view this rite of passage in a different and more positive light.

Allow yourself to get comfortable where you will not be distracted. You may wish to read this meditation and have it sit in your mind's eye, or you may want to voice record it and transport yourself there through the power of your own sound instrument within your sacred body.

Allow your mind to drift and float as you breathe gently and deeply in and out. Noticing your body and how it feels, drawing particular attention to your womb space and your heart. Allow yourself to get out of your head space and drop into the serenity of your heart and womb. Allow each breath to deepen and relax even more.

Travel back in time now by taking yourself to your earlier years as a woman, to the time when you first received your bleed. Visualise your mother with you (even if you do not have a close relationship in present times or do not know your mother or she has since passed); imagine a loving mother figure being with you and lovingly presenting you with a beautiful red flowing gown and moonstone earrings that have been passed down from her mother and her mother before her. Allow her to fill a bathtub for you with the richness and beauty of rose essential oil and red rose petals. Hear the water gently filling the tub and the warmth of the steam rising. Your mother lovingly leaves you alone with relaxing music that takes you into an intuitive trance-like state.

Allow yourself a moment or two now to honour your path of transition into womanhood.

You emerge from your bath feeling clean, soft, and pure of heart. You put on the beautiful gifted ritual gown and earrings, and your mother leads you toward the Red Tent. This is where the women have gathered throughout the ages for sacred talks, and it is now your turn to be initiated.

There are beautiful coloured candle holders outside the tent. Inside are lavish colours with Goddess paintings, wall hangings and statues of the Goddess in all her phases. You begin to hear the earth's heartbeat through the slow rhythmic sounds of native drums beckoning you from within.

Your mother gently opens the red curtains and invites you inside a beautiful temple space. The air is scented with incense, gently lit candles are all around, and there's a central altar decorated with a mandala of red roses, rose quartz crystals and angelic candles. All the women who have known you throughout your life are there—your grandmothers, aunts, Godmother (if you have one), mother's friends, and mothers of your closest friends, all who love and honour you for being the woman you are stepping into. They are all gathered to welcome you into womanhood. *Close your eyes and see yourself receiving this blessing as your journey into womanhood and into the essence of the times of the Red Tent awaken within you. You are loved, and you are so worthy.*

Aromatherapy Connection

Our sense of smell is the strongest link to our subconscious, and we retain memories associated with aromas for very long periods. Aromatherapy works through two main channels in the body: the olfactory system and topical absorption (through the skin pores).

Our nasal cavities have thousands of olfactory nerve cells that carry scent directly to the olfactory bulb (located at the back of our nose). The nerve endings then allow messages to be sent directly to the brain.

You may enhance your memory of ancient ways through aromatherapy, and a beautiful essential oil to do that with is patchouli.

This rich, sweet herbaceous oil has an aromatic spicy and woody odour. It is a beautiful essential oil for harmonising and stabilising the mind and has a hypnotising scent. Patchouli is also a great oil to allow yourself to get in touch with your body and your sensuality as a woman. This is an essential oil you either embrace and love or don't. However, suppose it is an oil you don't love the scent of. In that case, please tune in and see if there is a message within for you regarding where your feelings originate. It is said that scent travels faster to the brain than sight or sound and, therefore, can evoke deep memories.

This essential oil was brought to light in the free-loving sixties and seventies as an aphrodisiac. Patchouli has a beautiful message to share, allowing us to realise that to go out in the world and present as your most empowered self you must access the serenity and stillness within by slowing down to rest.

Remove the lid from your patchouli essential oil bottle and breathe deeply and fully, absorbing the aromas and allowing your mind to drift. Do this slowly several times as you ask yourself the following questions:

- What does my body need from me right now?
- How can I bring more rituals into my life to honour the woman I am?
- If there was an ancient knowing inside of me about my time in a Red Tent or Moon Lodge, what would that be?
- How can I incorporate the ways of the Red Tent movement and Moon Lodge into my present day?
- Is there a way in which I may connect to other women to share my experiences regularly?

Crystal Connection

By tuning into the offerings from the crystal kingdom, we can allow ourselves to travel back in time to learn from the past and infuse this knowledge into our future pathway.

One such crystal is that of garnet.

This exquisite crystal can be rich deep red, black, brown, yellow and even green in colour. It relates to all of our chakras. It is a stone that, amongst other things, enables you to connect deeply with your sensuality and teaches you to believe in yourself. Often women can get confused between the understanding of sensuality versus sexuality. The word sensuality is defined as being pleasing to the senses, which often can be sexual but it's more the expression of this physical enjoyment and how it makes you feel.

To allow yourself to sink into the concept of the times of old when you were an active participant, initiate, or priestess regularly embodying the ideas of the Red Tent or Moon Lodge, take your exquisite piece of garnet and hold this lovingly in your hands. Connect to the energy of the crystal as you allow yourself to absorb the ancient remembering. Find yourself a comfortable place (where you will not be disturbed) to lay down and place the garnet over your third eye (located just above and between the eyebrows) and actively call forward the ancient wisdom of old in the following manner:

1. With your eyes closed, quiet your mind through your breath, taking several deep and full breaths in and out;
2. Ask the oversoul (the collective soul or master of an individual crystal) of your garnet crystal to help awaken the ancient remembering within you.

"Dear Garnet and the oversoul of all garnet, I ask that you help me travel back in time to learn from my past and help me on my path as a woman today. Allow me to easily remember the ways of those that have come before me."

Goddess Connection

If I were to pick one Goddess that depicts the ways of the ancients, it would be Inanna (later cultures have also called her Ishtar). Whatever name you call her, she is the epitome of an ancient deity. She is a Mesopotamian Goddess of love and war. She is there to remind you of who you are at your core essence. She is fierce, assertive, deeply knowledgeable, with a strong independent sense of resilience. Nothing will stand in her way, and she fears nothing, teaching us that we are all her daughters and we, as women, can stand in our power equally. In her astral aspect, Inanna is that of Venus, the morning and the evening star.

By invoking the essence of Inanna, you are drawing upon ancient ways where stories have since been built upon lifetime after lifetime. Through the art of storytelling, the elders of the past shared their wisdom within their culture. The wisdom throughout the ages was shared among women within spaces created like the Moon Lodge or Red Tents. It was also shared within communities, both men and women alike, around the tribal campfire. It is that sense of community sharing that strengthens our sense of belonging.

Myths, legends, and folklore play out in history and have been of interest both from a historical point of view and from a mysterious and spiritual side. Invoking inside us the desire to understand where we came from and our cultural history both from an ancestral point of view and from a global consciousness point. Calling in a Goddess such as Inanna is a powerful source of connection to the ancient part that dwells within each of us and connects us to the bounty of all.

Call to Inanna in the following manner:

"Radiant, majestic Inanna, I ask that you be with me and share the ancients' messages, helping me retrieve the ancient qualities within me that will strengthen my reserve as a strong and resilient woman today. Help me stand in my power."

Affirmation

Use the affirmation below to help aid your awareness in stepping away from the busyness of life throughout the month and honouring your cycle as a woman.

"I relish the time I spend in solitude each month to honour my womanly essence."

Seed #5

Find ways to tune into your monthly cycle, rest and retreat from the busyness of life in the external world. Recapture the essence of the ancients by diving deep within to find the womb wisdom of yesteryear. Take practical steps to learn from the past and incorporate them into your life as a sensual, magnetic woman of today. Be an embodiment of the ways of the ancient woman in our modern times.

CHAPTER 6

Remembering Who You Are

The time during the global pandemic of COVID-19 highlighted and shared with me the understanding that not everybody you encounter will share the same beliefs as you do, which is okay. Life is about showing empathy to our fellow earth travellers and holding compassion for others when their views may not be congruent with our own. Deep in my heart and soul, I know that I was not brought back from India to go back to feelings of being afraid to be seen and heard for the woman I was born to be.

My near-death experience (refer to chapter 10 for further insight) hit home even deeper throughout the global crisis. I would no longer be on this earth plane if I were not meant to stand in my truth and help other women stand in their own light. We are in such a time on Mother Earth that we are awakening as a whole, looking at different ways of being and doing than ever before. A part of this is looking toward how our ancestors lived for answers to guide our future.

It takes courage to rise and be in alignment with all of who you are. This goes whether you are female or male. However, when it comes to helping the rising of women, which is where my light sits, and my passion is heightened, it is about accepting yourself for all of who you are, not just the parts that please others.

During the pandemic, I, like many others, have felt the pain for humanity and that we are connected far more than the countries in which we reside. This was when I understood even more that my calling to do the work I do—to be the woman I was born to be and show up in the world wholeheartedly—is not only needed but is vital for the evolution of humanity and Mother Earth. We are the stewards here to pave the way for the rest of humanity. Incarnating as a woman at this moment can be the most liberating, wild and free experience of all our lifetimes—if only we allow ourselves to remember who we truly are. During this chapter, I will help you connect with your ancestral roots to assist in your own ancient recall from within.

The women in our ancestral lineage did not go through various crises and struggles throughout their time on the planet so that we could take a back seat in our lifetime. They went through what they did *for* us and the line that follows suit. Their heartaches, losses, triumphs, and wins all run through our veins. They are on another level of consciousness, watching us like a television show waiting to see whether we rise or fall, but loving and supporting us all the same. No matter the story that plays out in our lives, they are behind us, cheering us on every step of the way.

As women, it can be easier to be *seen and not heard* or to have something we want to express but squash it in fear of judgment, whether it be from others or, worse still, ourselves (which is often the case and can at times be more damaging). I recall that in my teenage years in high school, I would usually shy away in class from being the one to call out an answer to a question. Whether the answer was correct or incorrect was irrelevant, as I would not want to voice it for fear of being judged by my peers. Heaven forbid I be seen as too smart, or worse, still be seen as a fool. These were my fears and insecurities projecting through, rather than the potential judgement of others. I felt it was easier to filter and merge into the background rather than draw attention to myself.

Suppose you are to be true to yourself as a woman, in that case, there needs to be an acknowledgement that throughout your lifetime and that of your ancestors, events and circumstances have created a wound deep within. These wounds have a profound effect and reside within your womb space, and left unattended can create blockages that prevent you from living your greatest potential and to your full capacity.

By no means are we victims, and by no means is having an ancestral lineage of trauma a reason to stop living your truth. Alternatively, please view it as a catalyst for change and an opportunity to heal the lineage of your past and free yourself and future generations from suffering. Start viewing your inner wounds as an opportunity for growth, for further healing for yourself and all of the generations past, and pave a light for future generations to follow.

When I first started ancestral healing work, I often encountered blockages based on fear. I come from a lineage of women stifled through wounds of the womb. In the past, women in my ancestral lineage have been silenced for traumas inflicted upon them by another. This happens far too often in our society (particularly when it comes to sexual abuse). Women are subsequently made to feel ashamed, guilty, unworthy and unlovable to themselves and those around them.

Any trauma that is held within the female bloodline travels from one generation to the next, much like that of an heirloom. Negative patterns of behaviour and a multitude of generational trauma filtering down the line brings about symptoms such as mistrust of others, insomnia, high anxiety, depression etc. Instead of facing the pain, it is often easier to push these emotions down into the womb, repress our feelings and block it all out by pretending that all is okay when it is not. It takes a courageous woman to make a stand for all of her bloodline when she says, "enough is enough", and she will no longer allow this trauma to continue any further in her bloodline.

This trauma may not even belong to us, and yet we feel the heartache of our ancestral bloodline whether they are known to us or not. This chapter will bring further awareness to these ancestral wounds so that you can observe and address yours also.

All the eggs that a woman will ever carry in her lifetime form in her ovaries while she is a foetus inside her mother's womb. This fact means that our cellular life as an egg began in our grandmother's womb. We are connected to our mother line well before our mothers are even born, let alone ourselves being born. This weaving of threads follows the line all the way back throughout time.

Broken down more simply, your mother created her eggs while she was still inside your grandmother's womb. At the same time that your grandmother nourishes your mother inside her womb, your mother is producing eggs inside her ovaries; one of those eggs was destined to become you! Think of it like a little Russian Babushka doll, each nesting inside the other. This is a mind-blowing concept but it gives rise to the depth of connection and power toward our ancestral line.

The food our grandmothers ate, her emotions throughout pregnancy, her thoughts and emotions overall about her life, her experiences and general health all have a part to play in our own life as a woman.

By reconnecting to our ancestors, we invite ourselves to reclaim our feminine divinity and release stagnant beliefs and patterns that may hold us back in this lifetime.

We each have this ability to tune into our womb space, witness from a place of love what is being held there, and then shift our perception of circumstance and move beyond self-imposed barriers.

Healing the mother line is an area that I am passionate about, and I have been witness to so many inspirational healings with clients (as well as personally) where they have connected to their ancestors to further heal their own circumstances, particularly within the womb.

My client Sarah, a mother of three boys to two different fathers, came to me to help her overcome her low self-esteem and fears of not feeling good enough. Her relationships kept failing, despite every effort to make things work. She felt she wasn't as good of a mother as she had hoped. As a partner, she felt she had failed both marriages and lost a loving relationship due to her low self-esteem. It was a constant repetitious song playing out in her life. Her boys were becoming teenagers, and she felt like she was losing them, just like she had lost other great loves in her life. Things seemed to be spiralling out of her control, and she knew she had to do something to overcome this.

It was not until Sarah started to work with me for womb healing, and regularly connecting to her womb, that she began to witness where her true wound lay and where these limiting beliefs originated from. After some deep dive discoveries, loads of tears, copious amounts of tissues, and establishing a solid connection to her womb, Sarah discovered that the real issue was her relationship with her parents. In particular, her mother, and how Sarah never felt good enough in her eyes. Despite a university degree and a successful architectural career, she felt she couldn't meet her mother's expectations.

As a child, she always tried to please her parents, competing against other siblings, vying for attention, and craving love. Sarah's mother passed away several years earlier, and the two women never really got to mend the rift between them physically or emotionally.

Sarah continues her healing journey but acknowledges that we cannot look outside ourselves to find the love we seek. This seeking often leads to heartache and heartbreak. A consistent effort to bring in more self-love allows Sarah the transformation she so longingly sought, and her intuitive abilities have deepened exponentially. Sarah now tunes into her body regularly, particularly her womb, through meditation (just like I have shared with you in previous chapters) and deep connection, and now feels content knowing that her mother did the best job she knew how to do, just as she is doing with her three boys.

Womb healing is a constant work in progress as we continue to heal both the micro and macro trauma within our lives and that of our ancestral line. Having the courage to keep working on ourselves and overcoming obstacles is where we truly step into our power as a woman.

Healing the mother line is a powerful tool to reach the next level of our true womanly selves. At times it can be a challenging healing process, but as a woman who wants to express the best version of myself possible and help my clients do the same, what I can say is that doing ancestral healing work is a way in which to give back to the lineage who help to shape the woman you are; this allows a way of paying it forward for those generations to follow.

Through my shamanic journeying, I have repeatedly faced the shadow side (the often dark and negative side of our personality that we try to hide from ourselves). It can be easier to decline the opportunity, but so much awaits us on the other side of fear. Allowing light to shine upon some of the darker aspects of our lives is where we can gain the most spiritual insight.

One particular journey allowed me to be the sacred observer, witness the lineage of women in my ancestral life (both known and unknown), and step into their energies to experience how life played out for them. It enabled me to see that this lineage of women, particularly in recent generations, was afraid to speak out. In many respects, I have felt similar in my life throughout various situations.

It wasn't until I went far back in the maternal line that I could find where my strength and courage came from and witnessed that further back in the line, the pioneers in my lineage were bold and stood up for their beliefs. Any battle scars were worn as a badge of honour to move forward and not repress into the womb space. This long lineage of powerful women standing up for their rights has been a guiding light in my life. They are now seen as ancestral guides to call upon when I need to bring more courage into my world.

"Don't ever let anything happen to her." These were the words of advice my grandmother gave me about my daughter in the final weeks of my grandmother's life. My daughter was three years old then, and we visited my grandmother together every week. I had such a strong bond with my grandmother from the moment I was born. She was one of three children, and she grew up to give birth to seven children of her own, followed by an extensive number of precious grandchildren and, at the time of her death, a significant number of beautiful great-grandchildren and one little great-great-grandchild.

My grandma was more than just a grandmother to me; she was a dear and devoted friend too. I recall how we would laugh together at silly jokes; she had a wicked sense of humour! I remember spending hours playing board games, and I loved the smell of the paints on her easel or admiring her pastels and watercolours as she went about her artwork.

I remember how much she loved the garden, both her own and my parents', and visiting botanical gardens together as her eyes would light up at the sight of a blossoming flower or the smell of a blooming rose. Much of my love for flowers, the garden and aromatherapy came from her love of plant medicine. I know she would be very proud of my garden and my fondness for the plant kingdom. My grandmother was an early maternal role model for me, and I wanted my future children to have a similar connection with their grandmother also. I am incredibly grateful that my daughter has followed in these footsteps by having a strong bond with my mother as I did with hers.

I still remember how my grandmother's hands felt as they held on to mine as we went for long walks together. In the final year of her life, I remember how frail her hands became as I would tenderly massage them with hand lotion that she always had nearby. Despite her ageing skin and her severe gout (a type of arthritis due to an accumulation of uric acid build up in the blood) that was evident on her hands, I still felt the strength within, as if she were saying to me, "I'll never let you go, you are a part of me and I love you eternally."

Throughout the dying process, it is natural for humans to go through a period of reminiscence and reflection as they review their life and all that has been endured. Although my grandmother's health was deteriorating and she was on a multitude of medications, she still had her mind and faculties right up until the late stages of the final year of her life. Growing up, I knew certain things were hinted at by way of sexual abuse, but it wasn't spoken about until she was going through the dying process, and afterwards, more came to light.

One day, she started to receive visions, which I now believe were visitations from her father (my great-grandfather), who had passed before I was born. Looking back upon what I know now, he was a troubled and disturbed man who did horrific acts of abuse that a person should never do to another soul. All the while, my grandmother had a mother who stood by knowingly and did nothing to stop these violent acts of sexual abuse by her husband and the father of her children.

I believe my grandmother was reliving the experiences she endured as a child and the silencing from her mother, and then in turn, her guilt and shame at the pattern of silence when this disturbed man continued the abuse with her daughters. In many ways, she sadly became the silent mother following a similar pattern to that of her own mother.

If peace and forgiveness is not achieved during one's life, it can often play out during the dying process. The agony of recalling events and experiencing nightmares that my grandmother endured as she was dying must have been difficult. I recall once visiting her in the nursing home, I took my singing bowl and helped clear the space of this negative energy. This was done before my training as an Elemental Space Clearing® Practitioner. While I understood certain aspects of clearing energy, I was not fully prepared as afterwards, I experienced a spirit attachment from my late great-grandfather (whereby his energy was negatively attached to mine). I then needed to clear myself and adequately close the split within my energy field. It gave me great insight into the power of energy and access to other realms and the importance of clearing your energy from entity attachment.

Seeing my grandmother clearly troubled and speaking words that made no sense (except to her) was painful to watch. My grandmother had several discussions with her local pastor before death, and the pastor was horrified at the events this poor young girl and adolescent endured at the hands of a so-called loved one. This was quite possibly the only time she ever shared her experience of abuse outside of the family. This was followed by her anguish at being unable to protect her daughters from this evil fate in their own subsequent childhood. These wounds over her lifetime had built up within her womb space.

When my grandmother was dying, the words she spoke to me, "Don't ever let anything happen to her", were not in regard to my daughter having mere falls and grazes in the playground. She spoke of stopping the act of sexual abuse that continued to run through the maternal line.

My grandmother spoke at length with me about how afraid she was of dying and what was waiting on the other side. We spoke deeply about what I felt I knew of Heaven, the angels and the Goddess energies that would be at her side. This poor woman was no doubt frightened of being reunited with her father, who had brought such shame, guilt, anger and fear into her life as a female. I gifted her a cluster of amethyst crystal for her to have on her bedside table. This helped to protect her as she slept with its high spiritual vibration, guarding against psychic attack and transmuting fear into love.

Throughout our discussions, especially in the final weeks of her precious life, she once said to me, "Kerry, how did you ever get so wise?" Looking lovingly into her eyes, I said, "Grandma, the angels will take care of you. Trust that when the time comes, you will be okay." It was not that I had *become wise*. I just knew in my heart she would be okay and that she would be lovingly taken care of. She feared death as she was unsure what or who awaited her. All she needed was reassurance that love will always prevail, no matter what we face in life or death. Since I was a young girl, my grandmother felt I was an *old soul*, I always felt an inner knowing greater than my years on earth. She knew I could help her, and she knew I could help our maternal line in the time to come.

I felt the pain, sorrow, shame, guilt, anger, disgust, and horror that all those before me had gone through. Sitting within my womb were those memories that were not even my own. Yet, they carried through cellular memory into my

DNA. My grandmother's anguish was carried throughout every pregnancy (including the loss of a baby close to term after her seventh child) into her children, especially her three daughters, who also unintentionally carried this grief within their wombs through to their children. Until such time as enough was enough, these wounds were to cut no further.

I am not dismissing those in my ancestral line who could not be as strong as their forbearers. However, there comes a time when somebody in the lineage needs to draw a line in the sand and demand that patterns of the past continue no further. It takes a strong woman to be able to do that. If you are reading these words, you may also be the woman to make that stand for your lineage. When doing this, you not only heal yourself of your inner wounds, but you do so in honour of those who came before you that perhaps were not in a position and did not have the skills or the know-how to alter their path. You are also setting powerful seeds for future generations that it is okay for us to have less-than-positive battle scars, wounds, and experiences. But we also have a powerful choice to steer the ship where we wish for it to move next upon the sea of life's travels.

Even if we are unaware of our biological bloodline, the energy of our ancestors runs through our veins. There is no denying this, and it can be used to serve us for the greater good of all.

Within my own life, I've helped to heal my ancestral lineage through regular connection to my ancestors in meditation, daily journalling, forgiveness, and acknowledging patterns of repeated behaviour—especially ones that continued down the maternal line. I have witnessed many of my clients who have similarly brought healing to their ancestral lineage by using these tools. Take a look at your own life and the experiences of your ancestors coming from the lens of love, compassion, and forgiveness for what they endured, as opposed to feeding the fear inside you. Think about how life would have been to walk in their shoes under their conditions and circumstances. We don't always know what goes on behind closed doors or what fears and wounds another holds inside of them that cause them to behave the way they do. Remember you are forgiving the person and do not need to forgive the act to set yourself free and start healing the pain you hold.

I understand how challenging this process can be and want to remind you that you are never alone on your journey. You have so much support, particularly in the spirit world, cheering you on from the sidelines like I am. In your own life, you can bring forgiveness to the negative patterns of behaviour or thoughts that you have inherited from your ancestors.

Within our womb space, we can connect to this deep and ancient wisdom to draw upon our ancestral lineage to be a warrior of our own times, on our own terms. This is what being a modern-day woman can be like when we start to view our lives as the sacred witness with the aid of our ancestors as one of our biggest allies.

Let's travel back in time together and consider your lineage that goes far greater than those you already know with the following journal prompts:

- What countries hold significance in your life, and how do you feel it impacts you?
- Where do your parents originate from? If you do not know, ask yourself anyway—subconsciously, your soul knows the truth.
- Do you have a love of a particular cuisine? Often there can be clues to our past through food.
- Is there music from other lands that evoke excitement within you?
- If you knew what your ancestors did for a living, what would that be? If you don't know, ask your soul.

These days, we have many ways to connect with our lineage on the internet by piecing together our family tree and collecting ancestral data, which can be a fascinating (and often time-absorbing) task. There are even ways to trace back our genealogy through DNA testing. You can go down this avenue yourself. However, there is also a place deep inside of you that already has answers to all your questions. Sometimes you have an inner knowing of where you came from and the kind of countries that hold a deep connection to you, possibly without having been there in this lifetime.

As for me, I have a love of France. Everything about the French way of life intrigues me. I love French music, French cuisine, French architecture and décor, and have a special fondness of French champagne! On my mother's side, we have French origins (hailing from the province of Lorraine), so this all sits well with me. There is English heritage on my father's side, and I equally love my English background, and no doubt Scottish and Irish too, which are both close to my heart. We are all intrinsically woven from threads all over the world, and as each generation goes back, we encapsulate an even more rich tapestry of life. We are so much more than the skin we are in today; we are a weaving of our ancestry and the lives the generations lived, on the lands from which they hailed. It allows us to remember who we are today and tune in and feel and recapture the energy of those whose blood runs through our veins.

We have the power within us to work with the spirit of our ancestors and our higher selves to eradicate negative emotions, limiting belief patterns and all that holds us back from living as our authentic selves and reaching our empowered potential.

Trauma, limiting beliefs, and patterns of abuse travel through our DNA into our cellular memory. This cellular memory that we hold within us is said to go back seven generations or perhaps even more, and affects the seven generations to follow after you.

The seventh generation principle comes from native traditions. The concept is that if you make any choice, personal or professional, you should consider how your choice will affect the next seven generations.

Technically, a generation is usually considered twenty-five years. A seven-generation healing calls on the people who came before you over roughly the previous one hundred and seventy-five years. You are the result of their choices, karma, thoughts, words and deeds, so you can go back to access this energy at any time, or place.

If you study DNA, you will find:

- You – 100% of your DNA
- Your mother – 50% of your DNA
- Your maternal grandmother – 25% of your DNA
- Your great grandmother – 12.5% of your DNA
- Your great-great grandmother – 6.25% of your DNA
- Your great-great-great grandmother – 3.125% of your DNA
- Your great-great-great-great grandmother – 1.56% of your DNA
- Your great-great-great-great-great grandmother – 0.78%, or less than 1%, of your DNA

Naturally, the same breakdown occurs on the paternal side also. Therefore, what you do today and your choices set the seeds for the seven generations to follow in your footsteps.

Accessing insights from our ancestors will help improve our relationships by alleviating conflict and bitterness that we can hold within the body and womb space. It can also benefit our physical, mental, emotional and spiritual health for those future generations to come.

Shamanic cultures worldwide have acknowledged the power of honouring our ancestors as a major key to our health and wellbeing. By working toward clearing the trauma we hold within our bodies at a soul level—especially our hearts and womb—we are also healing our ancestral lineage. In turn, we take part in healing the planet. In the following pages, I outline ways meditation allows you to connect with your ancestors to assist with this clearing.

We can often dismiss the daily life traumas of our ancestors—experiencing World Wars and living through times like the great depression—and what it must have been like for them. This all sits within us as the generations pass. Given our current times and the COVID-19 pandemic (particularly with so much isolation from others within the community), there will be emotional holding patterns that we will store within us for future generations to contend with. By looking into these emotions now in our current lives and shifting our thoughts and behaviours, we can address these in our life instead of carrying them forward for future generations. Let's act on healing now instead of carrying wounds for those who follow in our footsteps to deal with. We often haven't thought about why we react and respond to particular circumstances. However, thinking back to the times of our ancestors can give us a unique insight into our learned response to triggers within.

By remembering who we are at our core and where we come from, we can view life from the higher perspective. We begin to see that our core wounds are often there, not to be boundaries and barriers, but to bring us the courage to stand up for ourselves, to be seen for the woman we are growing into. The woman we want future generations to follow, to look back upon and admire the strength and tenacity it took to be who we are. You have the power to change your experiences through the choices you make today.

Below, you will find a powerful exercise that helps gain insight and understanding of your ancestors and how they may help you today as modern women of the world. Please note that if you are adopted or do not know your family lineage, allow your imagination and divine soul connection to guide you as intuitively and innately your soul remembers.

Please create an ancestral altar (on a table, mantlepiece or a dedicated shelf to honour your ancestors) in preparation for meditation. When I create ancestral altars, I like to also include a lace doily from my late Grandmother; you can do this if you have something similar that holds special meaning to you.

You will need the following:

- 2 candles: one representing your maternal line (your mother's side) and one representing your paternal line (your father's side)
- 6 drops of lavender essential oil (see notes in the aromatherapy section at the end of this chapter for further insight regarding this oil)
- 2 tablespoons of carrier oil (e.g. almond oil)
- Small bowl

Mix your carrier oil together with the drops of lavender essential oil in a small bowl. For this particular exercise, you will only be using a small amount to anoint yourself during meditation (which I will explain in the pages following), but the remainder may be used for aromatic dressing after bathing (either before bed that evening or first thing in the morning). You will recall we used aromatic dressing in an exercise in chapter 1 (you may refer back to this chapter for further insight).

Create a quiet, comfortable space to prepare for meditation so that you will not be disturbed.

Before lighting your candles, allow yourself to get centred by taking a few breaths into the body. Breathing deeply and fully and setting an intention for yourself that you wish to connect to your ancestors, use the following invocation:

> "I hereby call upon my ancestors and ask for their loving guidance and support as I connect into the lineage of my past."

You will then carefully light each candle, commencing with your mother's lineage, by lighting the candle on the left and thinking about your mother. Then, proceed to light the candle on the right and think about your father and his lineage.

Once the candles are lit, it's time to take your aromatherapy bowl and anoint yourself with the lavender essential oil. Gently place your pointer finger into the bowl and use a small amount on your finger to gently apply to the following body parts:

- Your third eye (located just above and between your eyebrows) which connects you to your intuition.
- Your upper chest to focus upon love and compassion toward your ancestors.
- Your belly button, to connect to your ancestral bloodline and genetic wisdom.

Once you have undertaken the above ritual, prepare yourself for meditation by lying down or finding a comfortable seated position, and gently closing your eyes.

Connect to the areas of your body that you have just anointed by using your breath to connect further and focus on your third eye, your womb, and your heart space. After several rounds of doing this, bring your inner awareness to that of your mother. Please spend a few minutes connecting with her energy, how she looks in your mind's eye, what she's wearing, and noting any familiar scents or locations. Let your imagination flow and make your experience as real as possible. When you are ready, you may intuitively ask her questions. For example, "What can you share with me about your life?" and allow the intuitive messages to flow in their own way without trying to over-analyse what comes through for you, just listen. Then when you are ready, connect to your maternal grandmother's side and then to your great grandmother and so on as far back in the lineage as you possibly can (remembering that you do not need to necessarily have known any of them in this lifetime, because your soul remembers).

Once you have had the opportunity to go through your maternal line, you may then proceed with focusing your attention on your paternal line.

When you feel you have reached a still point where there aren't any further insights, be sure to thank your ancestors for their loving guidance and wisdom, and slowly come back to normal waking awareness.

If you find yourself wanting to pause after the mother line, you may follow the same procedure another time to connect to your paternal side, or go deeper and undertake this exercise over and over again to connect even further to your ancestors and receive their guidance.

Be gentle with yourself through this powerful process, and take note of your experience in your journal afterwards to gain further wisdom and insight. Do this especially if things have come up for you that may need further forgiveness or letting go (we will discuss this in more depth in chapter 9). Be sure to blow out your candles with loving intent, giving gratitude and thanks for the messages you received and for their continued support in your life today.

Aromatherapy Connection

The act of anointing is to apply essential oils to the body (or to an object such as a candle, journal etc) as a way to strengthen your set intentions.

The aromatic properties of the oil act as a way to raise your vibration and keep your desires and intention at the centre of your mind. Remember that what you think about is what you bring about, and your thoughts are a powerful tool for manifestation.

In the recent exercise, I selected lavender as the essential oil of choice, as many can often relate to that of their grandparents and particularly their grandmothers through this specific oil of the plant kingdom. I know that it indeed reminds me of my own grandmother.

Lavender is an oil that feels like it wraps and cocoons you with love and comfort, supporting you as you connect to your ancestral lineage. The calming properties of lavender help relax any fears and inhibitions you may have about stepping into your ancestral past. It also enhances your intuition and brings contentment within your relationships with others.

Crystal Connection

Connection to our ancestors need not be difficult. Often, all we need to do is put out the call and our ancestors are only too happy to be at our side for assistance. Meditation is a wonderful tool to connect with our ancient lineage. Obsidian is one particular crystal I use as a potent scrying tool (to see visions). Using this crystal will assist you in furthering your own connection to your ancestors by creating a safe space to open up pathways to explore the spiritual realm and those who have passed on.

Obsidian is a hardened volcanic lava that has become a glass-like rock. It can greatly support you as you allow past hurts to surface, enabling you to surrender within and let the wisdom from your shadow side (the parts of our personality we often try to hide or deny) to reveal itself to you.

Hold your obsidian in your hand or lap while meditating to heighten your experience while simultaneously grounding the soul into the physical plane.

Goddess Connection

Our ancestors have come from a combination of different cultural and regional Goddesses over the course of time. Therefore, we each have a multitude of the Goddess within us, helping to guide and shape us along our path.

Call upon the Greek Goddess Mnemosyne, Goddess of memory and mother of the muses, pronounced (Nee-moss-en-nee) to help with ancient remembering of who you are. She is said to know all there is, whether past, present or future. She holds the memory of all, and was known as one of the essential building blocks of all civilisation. Mnemosyne is a particularly strong ally to call upon when you wish to remember all there is, both in the current day and the ancient past with which you are entangled. We hold all our memories within the cells of our bodies, some of which can be extremely painful, but all our life experiences teach us so that we may grow. Goddess Mnemosyne helps us to see that we cannot run and hide from our problems, and she gives us the strength to take an honest look at our inner wounds and face them so that we can start to make real shifts toward healing the future.

Mnemosyne is the daughter of Uranus (the sky) and Geo (the earth). She is the Goddess that you call upon when you wish to remember all that was, all that is, and all that will be. She is often depicted with a full head of long auburn hair. Far from just being a Goddess to help you remember your shopping list, she is one that rules the energies of the universe at large, the cycle of life, and the memory of how we as a society need to live in the world around us (a powerful message for our current times).

The ancients believed that at the time of our death and crossing into the underworld, we were given two choices: to drink from the River Lethe where all our pain from the previous life was forgotten, or to drink from the Mnemosyne, the spring of memory.

If you chose to forget, then you would be reborn and return to the earth plane and learn the often-painful lessons needed. Those who chose to remember would spend eternity in peace and harmony after healing from past trauma.

I bring this to your attention so that you may see that, similarly to the wounds you hold inside of you, you may choose to ignore them and bury them deep within your body and womb and ultimately remain in suffering. Or you may make the courageous choice to face the pain, remember the pain, heal the pain, and free yourself by living in peace and harmony like Mnemosyne.

Conjure up the spirit of Goddess Mnemosyne by asking that she work beside you, either during meditation or to assist you in your dream time while sleeping. Inwardly, call out to her by inviting her into your energy space. Below are some examples of how to do this:

"Goddess Mnemosyne, I ask that you be with me in meditation (or while sleeping) to help with ancient memory recall in connection to my ancestors and how they may help guide me with my life today."

After you have completed your time in meditation or upon waking (if Mnemosyne has been called upon during sleep) be sure to thank her for her assistance.

"Goddess Mnemosyne, I give thanks and gratitude for your help guiding me and release you of your assistance at this time".

Affirmation

Use the following affirmation upon waking each morning, allowing yourself the opportunity to look at the woman reflected in the mirror and help bring power toward your day.

"I rise with courage and strength, remembering who I am. My world is full of wonderful opportunities for me to grow and evolve."

Seed #6

Our life stories stay with us forever; by breaking the patterns of behaviour that do not serve you, the cycle breaks and discontinues. Be courageous and hold strength in knowing that you have the support of your ancestors behind you. You were born for the times you are now experiencing and within your DNA you are made up of a lineage of ancestors cheering you on to the next level of your rising as you heal the ancestral line.

CHAPTER 7

Awakening the Inner Goddess

Tossing and turning on a hot and humid summer night, my body was tired, yet my mind was stimulated by a higher source calling me to tune inward. I heard the call, and while I longed for rest, I knew that when spirit speaks, a woman in tune with the rhythm of her soul listens. This pulling and calling of my soul had occurred for a couple of days prior. In the early hours of the next morning, while the stars were still abundant in the dark sky, I rose, meditated, and channelled spiritual downloads. Within these spirit messages, some made perfect sense, and others did not. I still wrote these down afterwards, not with complete comprehension but with trust and knowing that in due course, all would reveal itself both to me and, once understood, to women worldwide. In the lead-up to my menstrual bleed, my intuition and womanly instincts heightened, and it was this factor that allowed me to heed the call and listen inward.

Just prior to menstruation (particularly, during the void) is often a time when women are at their most vulnerable but at the same time at their most aware, and the inner Goddess comes out to play and interact with the wild woman within. As women, we yield this strong power within us. When you hear the call, it's time to answer. You will be rewarded in ways above and beyond anything you could imagine.

As women, we hold the keys and wisdom of many lifetimes and the weaving of the great Goddess herself in all her majesty. An ancient remembering from deep inside us calls us back home to ourselves. Often during crises or transition periods of our lives, we take stock of who we are and where we are going. However, what if we were to do this every day, not just during those transitional times or when faced with life-changing and often challenging situations? The truth of the matter is that we can. As women, we may reclaim, embody and fully embrace our divinity and full magnificence of the woman we were born to be. A big part of this is allowing the Goddess back into your life.

We are in such a time where you can no longer afford to dim your light, and it is time for you to shine your magnificence into the world and beyond. It is time to remember who you are at your core essence and start fully living your truth.

From my work as a coach, healer and spiritual teacher and facilitating women's circles for many years, I have witnessed the changes and evolution that happen for the greater good when women start to honour themselves and all they can be fully.

A long-standing client of mine, Alice, was once a relatively reserved and quiet woman, often sitting in the background as more of an observer than an active participant. Over time she started to believe in herself again and began to see herself as more than simply a mother and wife of "home duties" and instead started to re-discover who she is. The understanding that beyond the labels placed upon her, she is, in fact, a woman of strength and a woman who started to wholeheartedly believe that she is worthy of having a life outside of the family home, she is worthy of spending time to develop her hobbies, passions and lifestyle. She is worthy of giving herself the love she saved and preserved for others alone. This re-awaking of the woman within has enabled Alice to pursue her passion for art again and express herself in ways she'd never imagined. It has helped her respectfully voice her opinion without fear of retribution or judgement. The honouring of her ability to own her truth has given Alice the courage to live a life that she truly loves and cherish the moments she has with her family.

The truth is the Goddess has been held within us as women since well before we were born onto this earth plane. We have brought lifetime after lifetime of ancient wisdom and teachings, and accessing this wisdom feels even more potent and prevalent in our current times. I feel the Goddess is slowly finding her way into the lives of women across the globe, seeking to find meaning and purpose and create a life they love and cherish every day. Often it can feel as though we gather glimpses of beauty, of precious moments in time, only to have these feelings dissipate through the busyness of life and the mundane daily tasks that we are to perform. What if we could go about life with a sense of admiration for all the opportunities that come our way and see life as the true gift that it is in itself?

Within each woman is a deep desire to rise stronger than we ever thought possible. When a woman starts to awaken her inner Goddess, she is no longer willing to listen to the part inside her that wants to keep herself small. Life can pose challenges, and yes, there can be heartache. That inner certainty to keep going and striving toward the most empowered version of who you know you can be will keep you rising despite the number of times you may fall along the way.

As a coach, I often see women with a specific goal or idea for themselves, only to talk themselves out of achieving it through fear. The fear we hold will always be there to some extent; it's a part of life. However, when you step toward fear and allow your inner critic to control your life, you prevent your inner Goddess from having her time in the light. When fears come up, acknowledge them, witness them, observe them and then push past them to keep striving toward your end goal regardless. The more you give in to your fears, the more resistance builds up, which prevents you from having the courage to keep going and achieve your desires.

When fear creeps into your life:
- Notice where it sits in your body (perhaps it's your heart centre, maybe in your gut or some other place).
- Notice any emotion that rises within you (e.g. anger, guilt, shame, embarrassment).
- Notice whether it has a colour or shape or some other description.
- Notice whether it has an attachment to an earlier time in your life, and if so ask this part of you what it needs from you now (we often need reassurance of safety and love).

The more you can process your fears and any triggers attached and bring more self-awareness to what creates these feelings within, the less anxious you are likely to be and the more empowered you become to step beyond these self-imposed limitations. The more you acknowledge your fears and any associated wound, the closer to healing you become.

Take a moment to go back in time and think of your early days as a young girl and see if there are any patterns of behaviour where you have chosen to play small, sit on the sidelines or allow somebody else to shine in your place.

When aligned with the true nature of your worth, everything falls into place. Life isn't so much of a struggle.

Indeed, there will always be times that are less joyous than others, but when you live your life in alignment with your truth, there is an inner strength that allows you to keep going. When you awaken the inner Goddess, she stirs inside of you an ember, a spark of magic that knows that even in the darkest times of life, there is always light. Your inner Goddess seeks to help you find it so the flame can grow brighter.

The stoking of this inner flame is cultivated within a woman's womb space; the burning and yearning to live your best life each day rises from this space of creativity.

From the body of work I am here to pursue; I know how much joy it brings me to see women gather together to share their wins and how lessons of pain and sorrow have strengthened their reserves to continue striving toward their goals and aspirations. Seeing a woman glow in her own light helps all those around her (both men and women) feel this emanating light also.

Awakening the inner Goddess isn't so much about becoming something you are yet to be; it's more about igniting the flame that has always been within you and cultivating awareness of all that brings you happiness, success and abundance, continuing even further along this pathway. We each have this ability to allow the energy stored within the container of our womb to flow from this sacral region and permeate throughout our entire body.

I know that one of my most challenging aspects of wearing masks during the world pandemic has been due to past incarnations having been silenced for living my truth. Masks can sometimes inhibit our identity. From the perspective of the spiritual masks we wear as women, hiding behind a mask can stifle a woman's ownership of who she truly is. As women, we often wear many hats in our life—a mother, a wife, a girlfriend, a lover, a career woman, let alone domestic duties we have as well. While we may wear many hats, women can also wear many masks, some of which are there as a protective barrier so that the outside world does not see the genuine and authentic identity of the real woman underneath, the Goddess that sits dormant inside of us until we permit ourselves to let her be seen.

We are at a pivotal time on this earth, it is vital for our evolution that we no longer feel the need to hide behind a spiritual mask and that our greatest strength lies in our ability to witness we are worthy, we are wise, and we are loved, and we deserve our place in this world. It can be challenging to put ourselves out there in society, to be seen and heard for all we are. When we begin to awaken the inner Goddess, we are in a place of inner knowing, which is cultivated by being true to ourselves.

Ask yourself, where in life have you worn a spiritual mask in fear of being judged, of being seen, of being isolated or some other projected fear? The act of surrendering to your fears isn't an act of weakness; on the contrary, it is a sign of great power that you are willing to look at these face-on and gently allow a part of you that is your pure essence to start shining through, for more to see and understand the real you.

If I were invited into your home, would your home reflect the *you* that the world sees? Did you know that there is a direct correlation to your home and yourself, they are reflections of one another. There will always be certain aspects of you that you may keep just for yourself or your loved ones, but overall is the person that presents on the outside the person you know to be on the inside? If your answer is no, or only sometimes, I will continue to help you discover, throughout this book, practical ways to reflect on the amazing woman you are and the courage to believe with every fibre of your being that who you are is enough. A woman who can show the world who she is, inside and out.

I believe wholeheartedly that a woman's power sits within her womb space and rises as the kundalini does from beneath the base chakra all the way to the crown and beyond. We draw energy in from the universe, it flows throughout our body, and we equally extend our energy back out to the universe. Life is a constant flow of energy exchange. When we allow ourselves as women to be in the flow of the creative energy held within us, we are unstoppable in our pursuit of happiness and fulfilment.

Within each of us, we have the power to shift and transform energy and access the innate wisdom and intelligence we were born with, to not only live with integrity but also to remember what we were born to do in this lifetime. This ancient remembering of who you are and why you are here is strengthened, and the doorway opened when we awaken our inner Goddess persona.

Who you are is not your body; you are so much more than this. Your body is the vehicle in which you travel in this lifetime. Still, it is a culmination of many lifetimes to bring you into the body you use today as your sacred vessel. A vessel that enables you to experience life in its entirety, a vessel that catapults you into every situation and choice you make and a vessel that brings with it an ancient knowing and an ancient remembering of all that you were so that you can live this life fully and embrace the person for which you are becoming.

I recall from my near-death-experience in India (I elaborate more on this in chapter 10) the eternal light and the love. This light comes from a place outside of us but simultaneously resides within us. We are all energy. We are in this world, but we are not of this world. It is this inner radiance that shines brightly from within each of us that ultimately comes from a source far greater than us alone, allowing us to be uniquely ourselves. It is this light that, once awakened allows the inner Goddess to stir more vividly within us and enables us to know, feel and understand that we are each placed upon this earth plane destined for greatness. It is in this inner knowing and cultivating of the seeds within our womb space that we birth the woman who was always meant to be. That woman is you, and that woman is every woman you meet and greet along your path. We are all here to help guide each other home to ourselves. It is within each relationship that we encounter that our lessons are given and our wisdom bestowed upon us.

Ask yourself, where is it in your life that you are dimming your light? It is time for you to acknowledge your greatness and shine your light even more brightly so that your pure magnificence may radiate into the world and beyond. I believe in you, and I know a part of you believes you are capable of so much more than you are currently showing. Acknowledge these aspects, witness your hidden strengths, and allow your talents to emerge. Permit yourself to tap into all the secret knowledge within you, and you will be amazed at the offerings life brings your way.

Our ancestors and the shamanic healers of the past used aspects of ritual, ceremony and spiritual tools to help bring about their wisdom. This wisdom is available to you also. It is now time for you to explore your connection to the ancient past and how you can embody the Goddess within so that you may be the most empowered version of a woman you can be.

Soulful Exercise

There is magic inside each of us, and it is high time we started to believe that we hold power to bring this magic to life. By bringing this magic to life we also bring peace and serenity back into our daily lives.

One way that I love to work with divine magic is through the power of a fire ceremony. A fire ceremony can be an extensive, elaborate experience through a bonfire. Still, equally, it can be just as powerful with a small burning bowl ceremony.

There is a certain feeling of awakening the Goddess within that I particularly love using with clients (and for personal use) with the aid of a small cauldron. Something magical happens when we release our emotional holding patterns into the flames through prayer and intention. By surrendering and allowing the flames to take what we are holding onto or by igniting what we wish to bring forward, it conjures up images of ancient times when women would gather to weave their magic and act as sorcerers to their own destiny.

In order for you to undertake such an exercise, you will need the following items:

- 1 flame proof bowl
- Several small pieces of paper to write on
- 1 pen
- Matches
- 1 candle
- Water to have on hand (as a fire safety measure only)

Allow yourself to get comfortable with the time and space devoted to inner connection, where you will not be disturbed. Ignite your candle and take a moment to centre yourself, and on the paper(s), write your thoughts and feelings that you wish to release. When ready, light the paper using the candle flame and then allow the burning paper to extinguish into the flame proof bowl. The power of your written word and intention will ignite and be transmuted by the flames, working its magic by surrendering to spirit within.

Do you ever wonder why you are attracted to certain countries or styles of clothing or the way certain women look or behave around you? Our cells and DNA are encoded with ancient wisdom from all of time. Sometimes elements such as the ones I just mentioned are a deep belonging to a culture somewhat different from the one you were born into in this lifetime and yet pulls you like a magnet.

During the downloading of channelled spiritual wisdom, I received in the early hours that summer morning (that I spoke about at the beginning of this chapter), I knew that I tuned into an ancient remembering of India, the motherland of the world. India is one of the oldest civilisations rich in culture and spiritual understanding, the land of yoga and meditation. A part of this land is within each of us, and we all have access to this ancient remembering if we choose. That early morning in deep meditation, I was transported to familiar lands and lovingly guided by a Goddess companion—*Goddess Hakini,* who shared mudras with me and ways to cultivate our creative essence and connection to sacred lands all over the world. My experiences, having travelled to India and throughout the Himalayas, helped heighten my connection. In many ways, India feels like home, but then again, I remember that home is where the heart is, and our heart and soul are connected and united by woven threads of energy throughout every land on earth and beyond.

During those early morning hours, Goddess Hakini taught me to remember the strength and power we hold as women within our pelvic basin. This sacred chalice is vital to all we can be in this world. Whether we are a young maiden, an elderly crone or somewhere in between, we all hold this wisdom within our womb space and pelvic region, which unites us as a collective whole. When we access and activate our power within our womanly bodies, we connect not only to ancient ways and rituals but also to our own unique essence and personal quest and purpose on this earth.

While I do not proclaim to have studied yogic traditions (although I have been a devout lover of yoga for decades, including during pregnancy), I fully respect the wise teachings and knowledge that those who have trained explicitly as yoga instructors have. I share my channelled insights from a source I trust, and that source is spirit in its purest form. Take what resonates and leave what does not; Goddess Hakini came to me that morning as I was open to receiving her call and sharing her teachings for the greater good of women walking the earth today. Together we unite as woven and connected threads of the earth across continents, lost lands, ley lines and sacred sites to heal, learn, grow, and evolve. Within our pelvic basin, we harness the power to fully awaken the inner Goddess.

Womb Activation

Allow yourself to get comfortable within sacred space. Tune out to the external world and prepare to dive deep within the inner realms. The spiritual exercises below will correspond to various chakras (energy centres within the body) and various sacred sites of the earth. Please note that while I offer you the sacred sites below, feel welcome to use your intuition when connecting to your divine self and see where your journey leads you. Remember that you are your own guru, always and forever. Use your imagination when travelling to these sacred sites and make it feel as real as you possibly can, give yourself permission to create.

While seated on the floor, allow your pelvic basin to open by gently widening your legs to feel a gentle stretch—in a seated, straddle yoga pose (see Yoga Straddle Pose diagram). Always stretch within your personal level of comfort, never push beyond your physical limitations.

- Point your toes directly toward the ceiling.
- Flex your feet strongly to engage the backs of your legs.

Yoga Straddle Pose

Gently and easily take several breaths into your body, particularly your womb, until you feel the dropping away of the outside world. With each breath deepening your connection, gently reach out toward your feet.

- Hold both big toes with your thumb and middle finger, with arms and legs corresponding to the same side of your body.

Do this for nine rounds of breathing (inhale through the nose and exhale through the mouth) or until you feel a sense of inner calm wash over you. You may undertake the above exercise prior to your regular meditation routine or as a lead in to the following exercises that will take you to a deeper level of connection.

The Stargate Connection: The Great Pyramid, Egypt

The ancient Egyptians believed the soul lived in other dimensions of reality, journeying to the stars and beyond. The Great Pyramid sits across powerful earth energy lines, creating a vortex. It is said that it stands at the exact centre of the earth's greatest land mass, dividing it into equal quarters of the earth. The Great Pyramid is also rich in ancient sound technology, so be aware of any sound frequencies that may enter your awareness also during the exercises below. Envisage yourself lying in the granite sarcophagus that sits in the Kings Chamber of the Great Pyramid. When I was there many years ago, I was able to lay in this very sarcophagus which held an extremely powerful energy. You may access this same energy simply through the use of your imagination and intuition.

Place your thumbs and pointer fingers together with gentle placement over your womb and pelvic region (your hand gesture should create a triangle, like we used in the exercise in chapter 1). Breathe deeply and fully into your womb for nine rounds of breathwork (inhale through the nose, exhale through the mouth, nine times).

With your hands forming a triangular composition replicating a pyramid over your womb, allow your spiritual eye to transport you to the lands of ancient Egypt and the sacred pyramids of Giza. The Great Pyramid is the last of the seven wonders of the ancient world and was built to face true north. This particular sacred site corresponds to the throat chakra. So, as you undertake this specific mudra, allow your imagination to sense the outer casing of the pyramids of limestone and the inner linings of pink Aswan granite.

Connection to this sacred site offers you the following:
- An awareness of the power of vibrational energy.
- Heightened consciousness.
- An opportunity to tap into cosmological energy.
- Reconnection to ancient Egypt.

You may undertake the next set of exercises in a seated position in either padmasana (lotus pose or half lotus if need be—see Lotus Pose diagram), allowing your spine to remain straight and in alignment.

Lotus Pose

Bring your hands together with all thumbs and corresponding fingers lightly touching in what is known as *Hakini mudra* (see Hakini Mudra diagram) to channel the flow of life force energy within. In Sanskrit, "Hakini" means *power* or *rule*, and by using this mudra, it is believed to enable you as a woman to have power over your mind. In essence, becoming and trusting yourself as your own guru.

Hakini Mudra

In the exercises below, I refer to specific energy centres within the body known as chakras. Below is a diagram indicating the location of the body's seven major chakras.

The Seven Chakra System

Base/Root Chakra (Muladhara) – Mount Shasta, California

While I have travelled to many sacred sites and lands across the globe and extensive travel throughout the United States of America (including a soft spot in my heart for California), I have not personally visited Mount Shasta. The state where I reside in Australia (South Australia) is known for its opal mines, in Coober Pedy. Mount Shasta heralds its own opal—a blue stone found near the mountain. I can only imagine the powerful energy it emanates heralding from such a powerful vortex energy space; allow your imagination to flow also. Think about Mt Shasta with its cascading snow-capped mountain ranges, rich, black forests, and hot and cold springs at its base.

Mount Shasta is one of the seven major energy centres of the world and has the second-highest volcano in the United States of America.

This site offers you the following:

- Access to all your hidden power.
- The ability to be one with the earth.

The lost land of Lemuria (a hypothetical lost continent located in the Indian and Pacific Oceans that is said to have sunk) is associated with this area; whilst you are in meditation, invite yourself to access the golden crystal temple that is said to exist in the fifth dimension (higher level of consciousness) above this sacred land.

In Hakini mudra place your hands energetically over the base chakra (a few centimetres away from the physical body).

The base chakra is an energy centre located at the base of the spinal column governing your connection to your physical body, your survival centre.

Sacral Chakra (Svadhishthana) – Machu Picchu

Machu Picchu has long been on my list of places worldwide that I'd love to visit; until then, it will sit in my heart, and I shall connect my soul to the lands in the realm of my imagination.

It is the most visited site in all of South America, with its air of mystery and magnetism. The area around this sacred land is filled with natural energy grids. Allow your imagination to envisage lush green mountains, sacred rivers and valleys. You may even visualise a Shaman in your presence or be involved in sacred ceremonial and ritual events for the solstice (where the sun appears to meet the highest or lowest position in the sky for the year). Allow this ancient land to speak to you and through you.

This site offers you the following:

- An opportunity to access shamanic journeying (connecting you to ancient teachings).
- Connection to the Inca lineage (descendants of the Andes).

In Hakini mudra place your hands energetically over the sacral chakra (a few centimetres away from the physical body). The sacral chakra is an energy centre located just below the naval associated with your reproductive system. It also activates creativity and pleasure.

Solar Plexus Chakra (Manipura) – Uluru

Uluru (Ayers Rock, as it is also commonly known) is one of my favourite locations worldwide. I may be biased given that I am Australian; however, I have a deep connection to this land, both Uluru and Kata Tjuta, which is nearby. I chose to walk the base of Uluru for my 40th birthday, and it was here that I received messages and profound insight for my personal journey forward. It also happened to be raining on this occasion which is extremely rare, and even local tour guides were taking photos with their cameras in awe of this magnificent image and rare phenomenon. The rainbow that appeared due to the rainfall was a birthday gift in itself (rainbows often symbolise good luck, wellness and happiness).

When you first lay eyes upon this substantial, rich, red rock, you can feel your heart opening and feel the presence of the ancestors and Dreamtime energy (how life came to be, according to Aboriginal creation stories).

Uluru is another powerful magnetic vortex and is said to connect closely to the heart chakra at Glastonbury, England (another of my favourite lands that I have personally set foot upon and perhaps why I feel the connection between the two so intimately).

When connecting to this space, you may sense the presence of Aboriginal elders, the mythical Rainbow Serpent lying at the base of the rock or even the sound of the didgeridoo playing around you. Make your experience as real as possible by using the gift of your imagination, as this enables your intuitive abilities to flow more freely.

This site offers you the following:

- An expansion of your personal power.
- Connection to ancient culture and traditions.
- The ability to tune into the mythical Dreamtime.

The solar plexus is an energy centre located at the base of your sternum that governs your digestive system. It is also the seat of personal power, your own inner sun. In Hakini mudra place your hands energetically over the solar plexus chakra (a few centimetres away from the physical body).

Heart Chakra (Anahata) – Glastonbury

Glastonbury, particularly the Chalice Well, is sacred to me; I cherish the time I spent within these sacred energies. Pilgrims travel from all over the globe to connect to this special gateway, and it truly does feel like the world's heart chakra. This area is also often referred to as Avalon and exists in a parallel dimension. It is said that this area was under water for millions of years, and there was an air of mystery while I was there in the winter many moons ago. The legendary King Arthur's energy is also prevalent at the Glastonbury Tor.

Many festivals for the *Wheel of the Year* are held in Glastonbury, so when you connect, you may feel these celebrations.

Wheel of the Year festivals include:

* Winter Solstice (Yule)
* Imbolc (Candlemas)
* Spring Equinox (Ostara)
* Beltane (May Eve)
* Summer Solstice (Litha)
* Lughnasadh (Lammas)
* Autumn Equinox (Mabon)
* Samhain (Hallows)

In times gone by, both labyrinth and spirals were often a part of Goddess worship and the whole notion of the cycle of life: birth, death and rebirth therefore, it is also possible that you may sense this energy too.

This site offers you the following:
- An understanding of multidimensional timelines (many realms existing at once).
- Connection to the Michael and Mary energy lines—invisible lines of energy across the land connecting to various churches, monuments and sites of interest. The Michael ley line is said to cross England from east to west; it is solar and has masculine energy, while the Mary ley line entwines and weaves around the Michael line and has lunar, feminine energy.
- A deep connection to expand your heart with love.
- Gratitude for the world we live in and our connectedness to the earth.

In Hakini Mudra, place your hands energetically over the heart chakra (a few centimetres away from the physical body).

The heart chakra is an energy centre in the centre of your chest governing the cardiovascular and lymphatic systems. It also has the ability to give and receive love, both to yourself and to those around you.

Throat Chakra (Vishuddha) – Mt Sinai, Egypt

The Great Pyramids of Egypt are known as the world's throat chakra, and this sacred site may appear with your connection to this exercise. However, as we have already explored the Pyramids in a previous exercise, you may wish to envisage the sacred lands of Mt Sinai. This land is also known as the *Mountain of Moses* as it is said to be where God first appeared to Moses to give the Ten Commandments. Allow your mind's eye to picture a mountain range of rich earthly red. St Catherine's Monastery is also found here. So you may also find yourself within the Monastery's grey granite walls dedicated to Mother Mary.

I share this sacred land with you as Goddess Hakini (in my meditational channelled experience) insisted that Mt Sinai be included in the teachings I share with you. It is one of the three sacred sites connected particularly with the throat chakra, along with The Great Pyramids and The Mount of Olives in Jerusalem.

This site offers you the following:
- Connection to the Creator.
- The ability to speak your truth and communicate with clarity.
- To strengthen your ability to stand up for your beliefs.

For the final three chakras, you will need to rotate your hand position in Hakini mudra by placing your hands energetically over the chakra location with your hands pointing directly up so that your fingers are reaching toward the stars (a few centimetres away from the physical body at your throat chakra).

The throat chakra is an energy centre located at the centre of your throat and is associated with communication.

Third Eye (Ajna) – Mt Fuji, Japan

Many people will state that the third eye chakra of the world has no fixed location and continues to move as the earth rotates. Often Glastonbury is quoted as being this location, with Brazil being one that next comes to mind. I would allow you to make your connection to the earth and your soul's calling to bring you to where you need from the earth's healing grid.

For others, like me, the volcanic Mt Fuji in Japan comes to my mind's eye in this chakra of intuition and profound wisdom. This active volcano is named after the Buddhist fire Goddess Fuchi.

My family and I travelled to Japan quite a few years ago, and I was mesmerised by the beauty of this tranquil landscape. The day we made the trek to Mt Fuji, it was raining, with heavy fog, and so the long bus ride toward the mountain base was in vain as far as being able to view it clearly. However, what was not seen by the eye was felt through energy. This is what I encourage you to always tune into—the energy that is abundant throughout our everyday life and allows us to tune not only into ourselves as a woman but also into the energy of Mother Earth and her sacred landscape.

Allow yourself to tune into the energy of Mt Fuji with its many Shinto shrines at both the base and ascension upon the mountain. Shinto is the indigenous faith or spirituality of Japan. Imagine its snow-capped mountain with perfect shape and symmetry. Whether your inner journey sees you climbing the mountain or simply being in awe of its majesty at the base, allow yourself to infuse in the energy surrounding Japan's tallest mountain, a beacon of mountainous beauty.

This site offers you the following:

- A gateway to open your inner wisdom.
- Connection to your spirit guides and your inner Goddess.
- Connection to the stillness that lies within.

In Hakini mudra, place your hands energetically over the third eye chakra (a few centimetres away from the physical body). Ensure your hands have been rotated with fingers pointing upward toward the stars.

The third eye chakra is an energy centre located between and just above your eyebrows, in the middle of your forehead, associated with the lower brain and pituitary gland and is focused upon your intuition.

Crown Chakra (Sahasrara) - Mount Kailash, Tibet

High up in the Himalayan mountains of Tibet, you will find a sacred site for many religions, including Buddhism, Hinduism and Jainism. Kailash is found nestled within six mountain ranges, creating the formation of a sacred lotus.

No planes, trains or buses go there, so any pilgrims travelling there must take all their supplies, and the journey is quite treacherous. It is said to be the *centre of the earth* and home to Lord Shiva. It is said that there are two underground cities beneath the peak. The mountain holds supernatural powers and is unclimbable (only one person has been claimed to have climbed the peak, a Buddhist monk).

Pilgrims walk around it, or some even kayak along its four major rivers:
- Indus (flows through western Tibet).
- Sutlej (the longest of the rivers-Northern India and Pakistan).
- Brahmaputra (flows through Tibet, India and Bangladesh, ninth largest river in the world).
- Karnali (a tributary off the Ganges cuts through the Himalayas in Nepal through to India).

With the above imagery in mind of Kailash, I welcome you to imagine a thousand petal lotus above your head at your crown chakra (sahasrara) as you enter the pilgrimage that so many people do from all over the world to this particular sacred site in search for purification to this mountain and its continuous snow-capped sides and sacred rivers flowing around. Myths and legends would have it said that there is a crystal city beneath the earth of this sacred site, so you may wish to journey here also in your mind's eye.

This site offers you the following:
- An opportunity to purify the soul.
- Connection to your higher self (your connection to a higher consciousness).

In Hakini mudra, place your hands energetically over the crown chakra (a few centimetres away from the physical body). Ensure your hands have been rotated with fingers pointing upward toward the stars.

The crown chakra is an energy centre located on the top of your head. It is associated with the higher brain and pineal gland as well as your connection to the Divine.

You may return to the above series of mudras and sacred site exercises time and time again for deeper connection to self and the earth around you.

Aromatherapy Connection

With all of the above imagery of sacred sites and lands across the globe and the connection to your chakras, I would like to invite the plant kingdom into your world for a deeper connection and appreciation of the land around us.

Balsam fir is an essential oil that I have discovered with great love in recent years, and I adore the energies this oil brings to the user. Given that I'm a southern hemisphere woman, it has not been a familiar oil to me until more recently. The easy accessibility of purchasing products via the internet over the years makes oils from across the lands so readily available.

Balsam fir is an essential oil that brings a sense of understanding the cycles and rhythms of nature and how this pertains to us as a woman while gifting self-appreciation at the same time as emotional healing.

As a woman, being able to honour yourself is vital to awakening your awareness of all that you can be and a fresh, vibrant oil like balsam fir certainly makes you feel alive both inside and out. It also heightens our awareness to the fact that we have both light and shadow and that as we age over the years, we still hold the beauty inside of us despite ageing skin and wrinkles that may appear on the surface. True beauty is more than skin deep, and balsam fir reminds us as women to accept who we are as a whole.

Place a couple of drops of this fresh, resinous oil on a tissue to carry with you throughout your day as a reminder to embrace yourself as a complete package.

Or use the following blend in a diffuser to waft through your home throughout the day (remembering as I mentioned earlier in this chapter that your home is a direct reflection of your life) or during your devotional practice to help bring your light essence to the front and centre of your mind.

Diffuser Blend
- 3 drops of balsam fir
- 2 drops of lemon
- 1 drop of melissa
- 2 drops of patchouli

Crystal Connection

Turquoise is a crystal that deeply connects you to your heart. Using turquoise is a beautiful way of honouring the depth of wisdom, beauty, inner grace and inner knowing that comes from awakening the inner Goddess. I love working with the energies of this stone, and I feel that you will too.

The ancient Egyptians often used turquoise in their jewellery while many other cultures also used this exquisite crystal, including the Native Americans, Aztecs and Mayans. Using or wearing turquoise brings you closer to ancient lands and times of old.

Goddess Connection

Goddess Sophia is a wonderful Goddess to connect to your inner wisdom; she has often been connected to Mother Mary and the Black Madonna. She is the Goddess Mother of the Middle East, and in Gnostic and Judeo-Christian traditions, she is the divine feminine. She is also the Greek Goddess of mythology. The dove is her totem.

By connecting with Sophia, you tap into ancient wisdom of all-knowing. There is a piece of every Goddess that is felt deep within each of us, but when we specifically call upon an individual Goddess for extra assistance, the energy is amplified. When you commence working with her, Sophia will assist you in finding your own truth concerning religion, long-held beliefs and finding the meaning within your own purpose and spirituality. For many, it is not until later in life, when motherhood or business/career duties have settled, that we truly engage in our spiritual quest to find who we are at our core in the deepest sense. The wisdom of Sophia is within each of us but often lies dormant until later in a woman's life before pulling this wisdom from deep within the chalice of our womb space so that we may honour the complexity and depth of who we are. We need not wait until the time of our cronehood before bringing in this wisdom. Since the global pandemic, more individuals are starting to awaken from their spiritual slumber. We are seeking a deep desire for connection within. Therefore, the time of Sophia's wisdom may be awakening within a woman's world earlier and with great anticipation for the help and guidance she may gift.

Affirmation

"I embody the beauty, wisdom and divine light of my inner Goddess."

Seed #7

As you awaken to your purpose and desire for all that you can be as a woman, life takes on an even more meaningful and fulfilling role within. As your beautiful inner Goddess emerges, the spark of light burns deeper and brighter.

By tuning into the awareness of sacred lands and sites, we may also deepen our connection to Mother Earth and all that she offers to us as awakening women of the world.

By actively awakening your Goddess awareness, a sense of clarity and reclaimed wisdom emerges—the wise woman within returns.

CHAPTER 8

Journey of the Triple Goddess

Deep within the recess of my soul, I felt the call to return to the lands of Ireland, to feel the cool misty air on my face, to feel the earth beneath my feet, to immerse in the mystery of the standing stones, to immerse among the waters of the holy wells and to feel the fire ignite my soul from the perpetual flame of Goddess Brigid.

Never before has a Goddess felt so strong in my heart, as I heard her call my name. I returned once more to the ways of old, the rituals, the ceremonies I had remembered from within the deepest core of my soul and had known so intimately in times gone by. It was my time to remember who I was at my core essence and bring this knowledge back to help women like you remember who you indeed truly are.

Several years ago, I did in fact, make the pilgrimage home to Ireland. I say *home* because it felt like a homecoming in many ways. I feel the Celtic blood in my veins, and recalling my standing on the lush lands takes me right back to times gone by when I knew I was a priestess, undertaking rituals and spiritual practices in many ways, much like I do today and share with clients how to embody and embrace the ways of the Goddess within.

My current day work facilitating circles and bringing awareness of the Goddess back into the lives and hearts of women in my community and abroad strengthens my connection to how Goddess energy can help us lead more fulfilling and accepting lives.

The Celtic ways restore my soul, filling me up so that I can be the best version of my maiden, mother and crone self, a tapestry entwined as one—as the triple Goddess.

Stepping onto Irish shores, I instantly felt a remembrance inside of me. I knew it was here on this sacred land that I was to reclaim the part of me that had forgotten what it was like to embody and embrace all of my womanhood. Remembering that inside of me is not just the woman I am today but also the woman of yesterday. Remembering that while I live in this moment as a mother, I am also that of my maidenhood and that of my cronehood to follow. All of these aspects of the triple Goddess lay woven like a piece of delicate lace embroidery, layer by layer, waiting for me to unravel them and reclaim the glory that is *she*—me, now and forever.

Come, journey with me to faraway times when the concept of the triple Goddess was easily and effortlessly understood. In modern day we can harness the power of the triple Goddess to restore our sense of hope, faith and courage for a life that is lived in wholehearted loving grace.

As I mentioned in chapter 1, my second pregnancy experience as a whole ran smoothly, all the way to the birth plan taking place the way I'd hoped. It was during my early years as a young mother coming to terms with the responsibilities that raising a newborn brings, which brought to the surface a whole host of insecurities and perceptions of what a *good mother* looked like. All this being said, there was a little trepidation at each milestone and passing each stage with a sense of relief that I was getting that one step closer to holding a baby in my arms. After our daughter was born, the expectation of breastfeeding was enormous. I had very much wanted to breastfeed with the concept that *breast is best* concerning nutritional value, bonding seconds after birth and so forth. As a mother wanting to go with the natural approach where ever possible, the thought of putting an infant on formula was not something that had ever entered my mind.

At the time of the birth of our daughter, the maternity ward was full; in fact it was over full, and I ended up being in a hospital ward that was the *overflow of the overflow*. The nursing staff were rushed off their feet, and obtaining assistance wasn't the easiest, particularly as a first-time mother wanting help with learning attachment skills and ensuring that my baby was latching on in the best possible way.

After leaving the hospital to go home with our newborn, and while still in the early stages of motherhood, I developed severe mastitis and ended up back in the hospital twice.

Mastitis often occurs through a cracked nipple (which was how it occurred in my circumstance), and the bacteria finds its way into a blocked milk duct resulting in inflammation.

According to Louise L. Hay in her book "*You Can Heal Your Life*", she has this to offer regarding the symptom of mastitis and breast problems in general "*a refusal to nourish the self. Putting everyone else first. Over mothering. Overprotection*" with the new thought pattern being "*I am important. I count. I now care for and nourish myself with love and with joy. I allow others the freedom to be who they are. We are all safe and free*".

I look into the above statement, reflecting on my own experiences, and know that all I ever wanted was to *do the right thing* to breastfeed and give my baby what I felt she needed. At that point, I thought I had failed her in this. Ultimately this responsibility of feeding our cherished baby became a shared one with my husband, enabling nourishment all around.

Within the first five weeks of my daughter's life, I was in and out of the hospital, experiencing excruciating pain whilst breastfeeding to the point where I dreaded feeding time. Whenever my daughter would cry to be fed, inside, I would cry at the thought of experiencing the pain and then ultimately I would also physically cry, desperately wanting the whole excruciating experience to be over (all the while feeling so much guilt about it all). One breast was a breeze to feed from, but as any breastfeeding mother knows, you need to empty both sides to avoid getting engorged with milk. I couldn't understand why some women found it so easy and just took to the whole breastfeeding experience so effortlessly, and then there was me! As a woman who typically excels in all she puts her mind to, it was so far off the charts for me to be unable to do what I thought was such a natural experience. Negative thoughts about myself would pass through my mind constantly. Women have been doing this for centuries, so why couldn't I? I pushed on through the pain; my husband would go to the grocery store and return with as many cabbages as he could find! There I would be, between feeds, with cabbage leaves resting on my breast to soothe the pain and hope to reduce the inflammation, but to no avail. I remember the cabbage leaves becoming so hot and wilted after being on my breast for only a few minutes, as this same feeling was created within as fever struck. My health deteriorated at a rapid rate.

The surgeon I had initially seen was not available to do the breast excision to release the pressure build-up of the abscess that had formed on my left breast. Interestingly as an aside, the left side of the body is often referred to as the feminine side, being the receptive side and representing, among other things, the mother.

Louise L. Hay refers to an abscess as *"fermenting thoughts over hurts, slights and revenge"*, with the new thought pattern becoming *"I allow my thoughts to be free. The past is over. I am at peace"*.

It is very interesting when I look back upon this to witness the hurt that was building up inside me was ultimately the hurt I was feeling at the thought of not being enough as a new mother. I was transitioning from my maiden self into the archetypal role of mother. Yet, I was not feeling ready, equipped or worthy of stepping into this next phase of my womanhood.

After suffering excruciating pain and being seen by another surgeon, I endured a needle to my breast with no anaesthetic to try to drain the abscess. Under the circumstances, my level of pain was irrelevant; all I was concerned with was continuing to be able to breastfeed my baby. Unfortunately, this was unsuccessful, and I was to return to the hospital again a couple of days later. In agony and excruciating pain, they did not want to admit me, given that I was no longer a maternity patient. Somehow, with a stroke of love and good luck from above, I was seen, and admitted. My original treating surgeon was to perform surgery on me the next day. My expectations as a young breastfeeding mother thrown out the window as my feelings of failure started to rise within. I'd felt I'd failed my daughter, I felt I'd failed my husband and even closer to home, I felt I'd failed myself. From here on out, unable to continue to breastfeed after my surgery, our daughter was to be fed infant formula from a bottle. I felt less than worthy of the title of mother.

How often have you felt similarly concerning worthiness (it doesn't have to be child-related)? We hold these negative patterns and beliefs inside of us where they self-destruct, lowering our ability to reach our full potential. Throughout this book, I give you ways to explore and see how you may overcome your unresolved pain and witness just how magnificent you truly are—and this magnificence comes from noticing the wounds you hold and bearing witness to the strength and lessons learned along the way. Turning negative beliefs into seeing your way out through the lens of a new perspective and paradigm.

I recall going to my newly formed mother's group with all the other women in the room breastfeeding their babies and me praying to God that my daughter didn't need a feed while we were there, as I was highly ashamed of feeding her utilising a bottle. Looking back upon this now, I understand full well that my self-esteem was low and had nothing to do with anybody else in the room. Truthfully, if I had shared my story with them, I would have felt nothing but full support. However, I was ashamed and felt guilty, and I didn't want to feel judged as a *bad mum* for putting my baby on formula.

The bond between mother and child during these vital feeding years is strong, and I didn't want to miss out on this. I discovered that I could still experience these beautiful times holding a warm little baby in my arms in the middle of the night or throughout the day. Watching as she grew, I would look forward to her feeding times and eventually watching my daughter grabbing the bottle herself and being swaddled in my arms. I also discovered the beauty of sharing this sacred responsibility with my husband. This opportunity would not be available if she were fed solely by breast. Grandparents even got to share in this feeding and bonding time, and the love was spread around, giving me opportunities to do other tasks when I was not the one doing the feeding.

There is so much pressure on young mothers to breastfeed. While I still feel that it's something I would have loved my daughter to have had longer than a mere four weeks of her life, it didn't make me less of a mother because I couldn't do so. The pressure we place upon ourselves as women are often far greater than the pressure we feel society places upon us. When you push down these emotions and uncomfortable feelings rather than dealing with them, they store in the container of your womb and negatively impact your life in various ways, including anxiety, depression, lack of self-worth and more. When facing your emotions, ask yourself questions such as:

- Where are these emotions and negative thoughts showing up in my body?
- If this part of me could speak, what would it tell me?
- What might it need or want from me to feel safe and loved?

Being a perfect textbook mother is something that only exists in our minds. When the reality is that our children receive what they need from us as mothers and caregivers, the bond created between mother and child counts, and when love exists between the two, nothing can break this. It all comes down to intention; where intention goes, energy flows. I learned to cherish my time feeding my daughter from the bottle. Instead of grimacing at the prospect of getting out of bed in the middle of the night or any time of the day and wincing in pain, I would get up and watch as a hungry baby grew content and filled with the nutrients she needed to develop and thrive.

While I still hold a physical scar from my surgery and breastfeeding trauma, this scar no longer penetrates as a wound to my soul. When a wound no longer triggers you in the same manner it used to, you can truly witness the depth of healing that has taken place. Instead of seeing a physical scar, I now understand the wisdom beneath the wound.

Many women on their road through motherhood may be able to relate to this or other elements of berating themselves as not being the so-called perfect mother or woman. The fact is that these children who come under our care are put under our love and guidance for a higher purpose than that which we may ever come to know. These children are God's gift; we are the caretakers until they can look after themselves. We may not always do things in a manner that we like but ultimately we are learning as we go, too. If we can give ourselves a break, take the pressure off of what we feel society wants of us and be the best mother we know how to be is all that counts in the end.

We are each given lessons along the path of life and the rites of passage that we partake in. We have learned from every milestone we have ever reached throughout our life as a woman. My lesson in breastfeeding, or lack thereof, was that some things in life are out of our control, we can have the highest ideals for what may take place, but in the end, some things are simply out of our control. Being a *good mother* has nothing to do with following the rules of what we feel society wants; it has everything to do with coming from a place inside our hearts that wants the best for our children and being a woman who accepts that we are all learning in life as we go. It's how we respond to change and how much we can accept ourselves and believe in our self-worth.

The high ideals that we place upon ourselves to achieve and succeed are not always attainable. When our expectations are not reached, we move into fear through guilt, shame, anger and so forth. These emotions, if not addressed, further add to the storehouse within a woman's womb. This storehouse can gather the heaviness and burden of the negativity, which we hold and then inhibits our ability to rise strong.

In my years as a coach and healer, I have encountered many clients who have felt pain and sorrow at the thought of never feeling enough. We are unlikely to ever speak as harshly to others as we can to ourselves, particularly when we are at a low ebb. When times are challenging, it's natural for us to bring the inner critic out to play and to even berate ourselves for the part we played in the situation. By bringing awareness to your self-talk, you start to bring focus to the words you use to describe yourself and the negative tone in which you speak. You can then make the decision to choose differently with your thoughts.

As humans, we go through various rites of passage, whether female or male. Often these rites of passage fall within significant milestones in our lives. As young women entering the time of menarche, we go from that childlike innocence as a young girl to learning to discover how to take care of ourselves as a woman with a new level of responsibility.

The Maiden
The archetype of being young and carefree. This transition from a child into early adolescence holds many facets of change, none more so than discovering the changes taking place within and knowing the ability to pro-create in the time to come and potentially bear children if that is God's will. This rite of passage from girl to young woman is the first of many in the lifetime as a glorious woman within. We may view ourselves as the young, carefree maiden, conjuring up images of long flowing locks, perhaps a flower wreath in our hair, out in a field of flowers with light shining down upon us like the sun's warmth on a summer's day.

Giving birth to a child may not be on the list for every woman for various reasons, or health challenges may prevent this. Whether we as a woman give birth to a physical child in this world does not prevent us from our own rite of passage toward motherhood. The triple Goddess aspect of being a mother still takes place whether it be bearing a child of our own, taking care of a child within our care or giving birth to an idea or creative endeavour; this is all a part of our rite of passage to the mother within us all. It's the nurturing side we have as a woman and the deep-rooted need to take care and embrace the developing nature of another human or the process by which a new venture requires of us. As life continues as a woman, we often long for a partner to join us throughout our journeys, share in happy times, lighten the burden of life's challenges, and learn as we evolve.

The Mother

This archetype embodies creativity and nurturing (both self and others). Often this aspect of the triple Goddess can see women sending all their energy in an outward direction to children and other family members and loved ones, to the depletion of themselves. As women, we cannot give from an empty cup. So the value of self-care is exceptionally vital for our foundational survival.

One of the following significant milestones in our rites of passage as a woman comes to us when we reach the time of menopause which has been discussed earlier in the book (in chapter 4). This rite of passage, once fully embraced, brings with it a sense of achievement, having reached the time of the crone. Along with the crone comes the wisdom of all the years prior, learning and developing and discovering who we are as a woman and finally having the ability to understand and come to terms with the woman we were born to be.

I like the notion of thinking of the final aspect of the triple Goddess as having two parts to the crone years. The first part is that of a *wild woman*, *enchantress* or *maga*. This is the first part of coming to terms with what happens throughout menopause and owning who we are becoming as a woman of the world. It's when a woman starts to have a deep longing to be seen and heard for all she is and has to offer the world.

The Crone

This archetype is one of wise leadership and experience, a far cry from the hagged older woman or spinster that society may conjure up these days or that of fairy tales with the wicked old witch. The crone appears in her wholeness, having survived the waves of emotion of all that the early wild woman days can bring up through our shadow self to finally awaken on the other side with a sense of receiving her much-awaited graduation as a woman in today's world.

Throughout our life as a woman, we consistently go through the above cycles of maiden, mother, maga and crone, not just throughout specific rites of passage. Throughout our entire life, whenever we embark on a new project, we go through these phases of learning, nurturing, embracing and embodying. The life, death, re-birth cycle of evolution can be put into practice with everything we do as a woman.

Reviewing your rites of passage and archetypes you have already walked through and noting how you felt throughout these experiences is a valuable exercise. It's also valid to look into those archetypes that you may not have entered into and witness what feelings are evoked at the thought of motherhood, menopause and beyond, depending upon where you are in the stage of womanhood. It can be profoundly healing to spend time in introspection, witnessing the areas that have posed challenges for you and even those aspects of you that you cherish and love.

These phases and rites of passage are here to teach us and to help us grow and evolve. We are constantly learning and growing, and with that comes wisdom, wisdom that may be imparted to those who follow after you. We are each storytellers of life, and women hold wisdom to share with other fellow women. Often when a story is told from the heart, you will be surprised at how many others have similar experiences or how walls break down so that free-flowing communication may occur. When we break down the barriers of our self-imposed patterns of behaviour and give ourselves the freedom to simply be as a woman, this is one of the most liberating and powerful offerings we may bring to the world.

Now is a great time to take out your journal and review your experiences through your rites of passage as I pose the following questions for your curiosity:

- How do you feel about your early years as a young woman?
- What were your insecurities, and do you still feel the same way in your current life?
- If you are a mother, what was your experience like with child-rearing?
- If you have not given birth to a child, how do you feel about this now?
- If you have not given birth to a child, what areas of your life have you *given birth* to? For example the birth of a business, the birth of a project, the birth of a book etc.
- What was your experience of menopause like?
- If you are yet to reach menopause, how do you feel about impending menopause?
- If you were to assess your life to date and look back upon your various rites of passage and the rites of passage to come, what have you learned about yourself?

You may be pleasantly surprised to discover just how strong and resilient you have been through the challenges, traumas and wounds from your past. While also understanding that you can change your thought patterns and re-frame to a healthier attitude toward yourself at any given moment.

Aromatherapy Connection

As women holding the sacred chalice within our womb space, the water element is extremely powerful (I share more of this in-depth in chapter 11).

Creating your own Goddess spritz with the aid of essential oils is one way to bring awareness as a daily ritual and awaken the beauty of the woman inside through the power of the plant kingdom.

In a 200ml spritzer bottle, add 100-150 mls of purified water, then add the drops of essential oil (I have put together a blend of the Triple Goddess for you to use, which mixes a whole myriad of delight for the senses).

> **"Mist of the Triple Goddess"**
> - 10 drops of orange
> - 8 drops of geranium
> - 8 drops of ylang ylang
> - 8 drops of patchouli
> - 2 teaspoons of witch hazel
>
> Note: witch hazel helps the oil and water combine and will help the scent linger for longer.

I have selected the above blend for the following reasons:
- Orange has a zest for life feeling with cheerfulness, warmth and joy. It also helps you as a woman not take life too seriously all the time and have childlike fun.
- Geranium helps you tune into your intuitive side while also bringing out your mothering qualities of providing nurturing and comfort.
- Ylang ylang emphasises your ability to be confident in your own skin and your passion for life.
- Patchouli is grounding and harmonising, helping you connect to your body through age old wisdom within.

Use this feminine mist upon waking in the morning to infuse your bedroom with bliss while understanding your connection to the wise woman within and all she has to share with the world. You can also use this before sleep as a means in which to infuse your dream state with the infinite wisdom of your inner Goddess.

Crystal Connection

Using amber is a way to connect to Goddess Brigid (refer to the Goddess section of this chapter for further information on Brigid) through the element of fire (given its golden brown and yellow colouring). Strictly speaking, amber isn't actually a crystal. It hails from a tree resin that has solidified and becomes a fossil.

Amber is a powerful cleanser for the chakras, allowing the body to enhance vitality by rebalancing and bringing about inner healing.

You may also be aware that many parents have been known to gift their babies amber teething necklaces to wear. My daughter had one herself when she was an infant. Suppose a child is to wear an amber necklace; in that case, it is known to be beneficial for the mother to wear it first if possible, helping with the bonding connection between mother and child. Amber contains succinic acid, which has been thought to have anti-inflammatory and painkilling properties. This acid is released into the body when worn next to the skin. As with all aspects of parenting, you only want the best for your child, so I am not advocating wearing an amber necklace for infants; merely quoting some of its suggested beneficial uses. Use caution and do what feels suitable and safe for you and your loved ones.

As an adjunct for meditation, amber is a beautiful gift from nature to assist in grounding energies into the body. It relates to both the base and sacral chakras. It may also assist in ancestral healing by dissolving patterns of the past that have travelled through the DNA.

Goddess Connection

I have a powerful connection to the Celtic Goddess Brigid, and she is often referred to as the triple Goddess. I believe that if we as women were more able to understand the ways of the Goddess and how she may assist us through life as women as she would in ancient times, we would be far better suited to deal with life's trials and tribulations.

One cool, frosty morning around the winter solstice, my family and I set off in search of County Kildare, where we were to meet with the *Brigidine Sisters* (a congregation of nuns) at *Solas Bhride* (which means Brigid's light or flame). Solas Bhride and Hermitages is a beautiful spiritual centre right in the heart and soul of Brigid of Kildare. This is a popular destination where pilgrims gather from across the globe to connect to the values and customs associated with St Brigid. Brigid's flame has been lovingly tended and looked after in Solas Bhride since it was again relit in 1993. Brigid's flame acts as a light of hope, peace and justice for our world.

Given the time of year we arrived, we were extremely fortunate to have spent time with the nun's before preparations ahead of Christmas festivities. At this time, they are normally closed, but given our length of travel to be there and having contacted them ahead of time, the nun felt, on a deep level, that we needed to be there. It had also been winter solstice, so the facility's energy was still palpable from pilgrims having gathered in meditational practice the evening prior. After my *seed* candles were lit (from the perpetual flame), the nun took us on a powerful meditation journey to connect to the breathtakingly beautiful energy of Brigid.

I walked the holy labyrinth within the grounds. I held my clear quartz generator crystal toward the sun to charge as I brought the sun's rays and Goddess Brigid's light into my energy field and that of my special quartz crystal. This quartz crystal generator travels with me all over the globe. It has been to some of the most sacred sites worldwide and therefore holds immense power and activation for me.

We then journeyed within the quaint town of Kildare to two of Brigid's sacred wells to gather holy water to bring home to Australia and to further immerse in the tranquillity.

Goddess Brigid (who is known by many names: Brigit, Brig, Bride, Brigantia, Saint Brigid and Mary of the Gael), as well as being the Goddess of the sacred flame, is also the Goddess of poetry, healing and smithcraft. She is a Goddess of hearth, home and Goddess of fire, and water. She is the keeper of the holy wells, the rivers of healing, and igniting creativity through her flames of light. At her shrine at Kildare, there was previously kept a perpetual flame by 19 of her priestesses. The nuns of the Abbey have since tended to this same flame in Kildare after the Christianisation of Ireland. In my home, I have a small bowl of water at my front door dedicated to Goddess Brigid. I also have a dedicated candelabra in her honour. The candle is lit from a seed candle I brought back from Solas Bhride, Kildare. Whenever it is lit, I use the following phrase:

"In Brigid's name, I light my flame."

The above phrase is a line I continue to use every time I ignite the flame of a candle; it is a part of bringing the sacred into a daily ritual.

In ancient times, priestesses would gather to tend to Brigid's perpetual flame in Kildare at the original site of a wooden church built around 470 A.D. where Brigid established a monastery. The perpetual flame burned until the mid-16th century. Given the time of year we as a family visited this site, there wasn't a great deal open by means of extra learning from local guides or tourism information. However, I believe some of the best forms of education are the discoveries we feel in the presence of sacred sites and the remembrance it invokes inside us. As women, we have this ancient remembrance held within the container of our womb. All the creation we could ever ask for is available to us upon the drawing of the waters within our sacred chalice.

Driving away from Kildare, I felt a sense of peace wash over me like I had come full circle. I was full of excitement and anticipation; I was full of creativity for all the seeds I was to plant inside of me for the future births of new endeavours.

It has been said that Goddess Brigid leans over every cradle to watch over our children. The same can be said for calling her to watch over every project we are birthing into the world. As Brigid is connected to health and fertility, it makes perfect sense that we as women get to know Brigid in our own way and to see how she may assist us in becoming fertile in the sense of all the new life we may wish to bring into this world, be it children or projects of the heart. We can use her fire of inspiration to ignite the creative spark residing within the womb to give rise to all we can be.

Soulful Connection

As Goddess Brigid is the Goddess of poetry, try your hand at writing your very own *name poem*. A name poem can be used in prayer, meditation, as a mantra or as your personalised affirmation.

It is a way to honour and embody yourself as a woman—your past, present and future self.

Consider the attributes and qualities that you possess that you would like to share if you were to meet someone for the first time. What might you want them to know about you at your core essence? What are your positive traits and special qualities that make you uniquely you? Who are you at your core essence?

Complete this sentence to start on your journaling process to discover more of you:

I am a woman of …

For example: I am a woman of … loyalty, trust, courage, guidance, dependability, hardworking, honesty, wisdom etc.

Once you have created your list of words that feel like you (the you on the inside, the *real* you), start to get curious and think about the turning points in your life so far. Turning points are events that have helped to shape who you are today e.g. marriage, divorce, the birth of children, the loss of children and loved ones, occupations, education etc). Turning points help to create change in direction from experiences and moments in your life; they are the defining ways that shape you moving forward particularly as we move from one rite of passage of womanhood to another.

Once you have your list of turning points, it is time to call upon Goddess Brigid to assist you in allowing your creative inspiration to flow and write your name poem.

Call to Goddess Brigid in a quiet space in the following manner:

"I call upon Goddess Brigid as the Goddess of poetry, and ask for your support, guidance and love as I look back upon the turning points in my life so that I may write my name poem from a place of non-judgement."

The key here is to sit in the space of non-judgement, use the words that describe you and use your turning points to express the lessons learned.

This soulful exercise can be compelling in bringing awareness to your inner growth. It is not until we look back and witness how we felt at certain times in our life and how we responded that we acknowledge either how far we have come or where we may need to do a little more healing and forgiveness to self.

These were some of my own words to share as an example:

Loyal, honest, trustworthy, good listener, guidance, caring, hardworking, reliable, dependable, deep thinker, wise old soul, frightened of judgment.

I used the following turning points to create my name poem:

Marriage, miscarriage, the birth of my daughter, death of my grandmother and my near-death experience.

Writing my name poem, I witnessed where I had felt small and where I was hiding in the shadows of fear. I was able to observe through my words the strength that comes from loving all of who you are as a woman. There may be times when life brings significant challenges and hardship and your womb aches, but just as quickly as those rose petals in the garden of your womb drop away, rebirth continues as in the springtime new life, and new hope is created within.

Do not be afraid of how your poem is written or even the tenses; you are not in an English class now, you are writing from your heart and soul, and nobody needs ever read your prose. There is such profound power in the written word. Nobody needs to read this but you if you so choose. You may even find that the words flowing onto the page occur while you are in channel; some words may not even be words you may use in the current day, and yet your soul knows you and knows what to scribe. Be true to yourself and write your poem with the aid of Goddess Brigid, knowing that you are and always have been more than enough.

Affirmation

"I ignite the fire of the triple Goddess to spark inspiration within me, now and forevermore."

Seed #8

As a woman, we weave the aspects of the triple Goddess through our veins. Bringing deep awareness to your past through life's turning points allows you to ignite the fire within you and keep these fires burning so that the maiden, the mother and the crone all flourish with honesty and love.

CHAPTER 9

The Path of Forgiveness

Some acts in life are horrific, painful, immoral and inhumane, to say the least; however keeping hold of the anger, grief, sadness and bitterness within only keeps you a prisoner within your own body and soul.

The ability to set yourself free from this pain and anguish is not an easy task and should not be taken lightly by any means.

You do not need to forgive the act, for some actions within society are beyond comprehension. However, to heal and move forward, bringing forgiveness to the person or people involved allows you to free yourself from internal turmoil.

In your quest for forgiveness, it all comes down to divine timing and your willingness to do so. When the body, mind and spirit are ready to forgive and surrender within, it will. We cannot force things to happen before we are ready. Allow yourself the ability to be kind to yourself. Some wounds go deeper than others which may also mean that some areas of your life that require forgiveness may take a little longer, and that's okay. Wherever you are on your path to forgiveness is where you need to be right now.

So often, we are tough on ourselves and allow our *shoulds* to take over. "I should forgive this person"—the truth is that even if we know that forgiveness will ultimately set us free if we are not ready, we are not ready. We need to feel it in our heart space with deep genuine love. Ultimately we are all children of the light, and sometimes darkness takes over, but deep at our core we are still made of the purest light essence. There is no place where others start, and we stop; ultimately, we are all in the same light. It is the light inside of us that allows us to surrender and feel at peace with ourselves through the act of forgiveness.

Forgiveness sets us free so that we are no longer attached to the emotion involved in the act. Being able to forgive others also allows us to forgive ourselves in the process. You may not be able to forget, but you have the opportunity to forgive, which will enable you to move forward with grace and humility and keeps your light stronger toward your future.

As I mentioned, we all go through different stages of readiness and willingness regarding forgiveness. If you are reading this and it stirs something inside you, bringing up emotions of anger, guilt, shame, denial or some other emotion—that's okay. It's a process that requires a deep dive into the shadow self, which can be a little scary but will ultimately feed your soul to a life of inner freedom. The key is in the timing. When you are ready, healing will occur, and forgiveness will proceed. Until then, be gentle with yourself and know that you are at varying degrees of change and healing, and it comes down to divine timing.

In my life, there have been many situations where I have had to look at my inner wounds and forgive those in my life where pain was inflicted, intentional or otherwise. I've understood that as hard as these wounds have been, they have also enabled me to heal at a soul level. I wouldn't be the teacher I am today without having walked through these internal flames myself.

One of the biggest keys to forgiveness is through prayer. To be able to pray for those who may have harmed us may seem outrageous at first. Still, ultimately we are also giving ourselves freedom through forgiveness. We also open ourselves up to receive more divine light from the universe. When we place our intention on allowing the light of the divine to work through us and help us to help others through the act of forgiveness, it opens doorways of endless possibilities. In the beginning, it can be a real challenge, it may be difficult, but the more you practice the act of forgiveness, the easier it becomes until it encompasses your way of being in the world. Your willingness to forgive is the first action step forward.

There is enormous power in sitting with an emotion, but the key is to avoid being stuck in the emotion for too long. Emotions are energy-in-motion; therefore, they need to keep moving and not remain stagnant, as that will lead you off course.

Allowing yourself to sit there with anger, bitterness, and toxicity keeps you as a prisoner within your own body. It can often contribute to conditions and disease. There is a strong link between our metaphysical conditions and our emotions. As mentioned in an earlier chapter, Louise L. Hay has an outstanding book called *You Can Heal Your Life*, and within it, there is a section based purely on the metaphysical components of conditions and how they may potentially weave into our lives as diseases. In my work as a coach and healer, I have often consulted this book with clients, and the correlation between the two has been phenomenal.

In my own life, I experienced a deep wound, regarding my longing for another child to join our family of three. For years I held the inner pain and longing for a sibling for our daughter. Other pregnant women would constantly surround me. Some would say things like, "Oh, when are you going to have another one?" Sentences like this were like a dagger to my heart. It wasn't that I couldn't have another child; we chose not to as a married couple. Although, if the truth were told I held it inside of me for years that it wasn't really *my* choice, it was my husband's. I now understand that it was a decision we both made for the greater good. Perhaps my husband was more in tune with this divinity than I was because the desire for another baby blindsided me. Many a tear was shed behind closed doors at my anguish, desire and longing for another child. Eventually, this deep longing and bitterness at the circumstances surrounding our decision led to the formation of a large fibroid mass that developed in my uterus.

I remember being at a Hay House *I Can Do It Conference* in 2013 being in the presence of Doreen Virtue and receiving a message from spirit that "my desire for children is not mine at this time". I also recall a trip to Hong Kong even earlier than this in 2011 at Wong Tai Sin Temple, where I undertook the old tradition of fortune telling via joss sticks. Joss sticks is an ancient tradition of shaking a cylinder filled with sticks with corresponding numbers. When one falls out, it relates to a prediction read by a soothsayer nearby the temple. This precise prediction related to my desire for another baby, and the soothsayer predicted that I would only have one child in this lifetime. I remember throwing out the prediction and being angry at the result, feeling that the whole thing was nothing short of a fraud. I remember my husband saying it was my choice to do the reading, and I didn't like what I heard. That simple act of the joss stick tradition in Hong Kong stayed with me for many years, and I was not too fond of the outcome. I was outraged by it; it stirred up such deep emotional anger, adding to the boiling pot brewing unknowingly within my womb.

Many years would unfold, and the decision not to add to our family of three was solidified. In some ways I had accepted it, but there was still a part of me that held on to the hurt and some of this hurt was directed at my ever-loving and supportive husband.

It was the winter of 2017 when my doctor discovered a potential abnormality during a routine pap smear and gynaecological exam and sent me off for further investigation. An initial external ultrasound showed a rather large fibroid mass on the inner lining of my uterus. I was to follow up in a week with an internal ultrasound for more definitive results. I had been suffering from irregular periods in recent months. I felt my hormones were all over the place, which was the primary catalyst for seeing my doctor in the first place.

During this week-long wait, I undertook deep soul-searching and in-depth conversations with my husband. My biggest fear was that my uterus would be removed and I would require a hysterectomy. I felt I had healed so much, particularly in recent years, by coming to terms with the loss of potentially giving birth to future children. I began to realise that the deep wound I'd carried within me for years was becoming a physical barrier I needed to remove to move forward with my life. The decision to no longer have any more children was no longer a part of the person I was stepping into. I was okay with that, but I also had one final aspect to work on—forgiveness.

I'd long held onto the pain that I felt I wasn't as good a mother as I'd wanted to be to my daughter. There was such a lot going on in my daughter's early child rearing (we were extensively renovating our home, we were also sub-dividing and developing two investment properties, my husband and I were running three businesses, trying to navigate vexatious legal disputes, I was also dealing with the grief following my grandmother's passing, as well as other stress factors of general day to day life). All of this, on top of my husband being involved in a major car accident that threatened his life and resulted in physical pain from the injuries and mental and emotional stress. Looking back upon it now, it shows the extent of our love for one another as husband and wife and our love for our daughter to remain united throughout this tumultuous and often turbulent time in our lives.

All I'd ever wanted was to be a mother. Yet, I felt I was a mother second to everything else around me when my deepest desire was to be a mother fully and completely. I felt that to take my uterus from me would be a cruel way of yet again removing my right of choice. In that week, between ultrasounds, I brought forgiveness toward my husband for his part in what I felt at the time was taking my right to motherhood away. At that time, I also forgave myself for my feelings of lack regarding being the best mother I could be. Ultimately, I did the best I could under the stressful circumstances we were in at the time and at no time was my love not expressed toward my family.

The results of my internal ultrasound came back completely clear. I was free from all pain, and I was also free of the past. However, the MRI results from one week to the next were conflicting. The doctor mentioned the fibroid mass was visible one week, then not the next, as if it were a miracle. I went for a second opinion with a different radiologist to be sure and put my mind at ease.

Sitting in the hospital waiting room for my results was one of my life's most nerve-wracking times. I chose to go there alone; I felt it was my healing and wanted to receive the results myself. I remember having the results in my hand and not opening the letter until in the car park. I prayed so hard, and tears streamed sobbingly down my face as I opened to see the following words:

Conclusion: There is no evidence of adenomyosis. No fibroid is demonstrated. Both ovaries were of standard size.

This was one of the longest ten days of my life. What I discovered from all of it was my belief in the power that made the body heals the body and that the power of the mind and prayer can help overcome any obstacles and allow space for miracles to occur.

If you have symptoms of any kind with the body, it is always best to get them checked out by a healthcare professional and not ignore them. However, there is always an aspect worth looking into, and that is the metaphysical component of how the condition was created in the first place.

During that time of my life, reviewing my thought patterns and how I may have contributed to this condition, I also looked into the association with fibroids. According to Louise L. Hay's list, the probable cause of fibroids was *"nursing a hurt from a partner. A blow to the ego",* with the new thought pattern being *"I release the pattern in me that attracted this experience." "I create only good in my life".*

Wow, I thought to myself! There is no denying the truth to yourself about your life, and when the truth stares you right in the face, there really is no denying it. When I read that line about nursing a hurt from a partner, I knew instantly it had to do with harbouring the pain of feeling like I had no choice regarding the path of future pregnancy and motherhood. All those years, deep inside, I held pain and hurt from something I felt my husband inflicted upon me. When the fact is, we always have choices in life. The decision was a mutual one, although I was not prepared to have admitted that to myself during those years of anguish. My love for my husband and our daughter was more potent than my desire for another child. When I think about it now, I sit in reflection of the void I was trying to fill by means of another child, when in fact, there is nothing an outside influence can fill to make you feel whole and complete. The feeling of being complete is an inside job, and a massive part of that comes under the banner of forgiveness. It's a move closer to love and away from fear that fills any void, and ultimately that love needs to be one of self-love.

I will ask you to pause and get curious about where in your life you are trying to fill a void through outside influence. Where are you potentially harbouring hurt from somebody or something else and feeling like you have no control? Step closer toward accepting the situation and forgiving those you may blame, and even more importantly, bring forgiveness to yourself for your part in the story.

Looking into the metaphysical components of fibroids, taking a deep dive into my attached emotions, and releasing myself through forgiveness changed the medical outcome. How else can a large fibroid mass and pain be present one day and completely disappear within a couple of weeks as if never there in the first instance? Miracles happen when we step out of our own way and let the magic of the divine work through us.

If we close our hearts to the concept of forgiveness, we also close off the possibility of new ways of being in our lives. We all receive the same download from spirit relating to the power of forgiveness, but some of us keep that download in storage while others embrace it, heal from it and change the trajectory of their lives.

Are you ready to take the first step toward forgiveness?

You cannot experience the beauty within your womanly essence when you are holding on so tightly to the pain of suffering. It takes courage to descend deep within, but when it's time, you may truly awaken the fullness of the expression of you.

I have seen many women throughout my years as a coach, healer and spiritual teacher who have held onto pain by blaming others for their situation and not taking ownership of their part. Relationships are a two-way street, and every union we enter, whether romantic or otherwise, holds lessons for each of us. People come into our lives that challenge us and ultimately help us grow somehow. Relationships are not always easy and smooth sailing, but holding onto a grudge, anger, resentment, jealousy, and other negative emotions impacts your body, mind and spirit in some shape. Often this may contribute toward ill health, and I encourage you to stop the blame game and take ownership of the situation. Life is about choices; sometimes, we may not necessarily take the right one at the time, but we can always come back later and admit that perhaps we didn't handle things as best we could. We could view the situation from a different and higher perspective. We may not always be right, even when we think we are. Accepting that we are capable of mistakes and accepting that it's easier to blame others than take the higher ground is all a part of discovering who we are at our core. By forgiving others for their role in the story you signed up to and forgiving yourself is one of the most liberating and freedom-seeking pathways you may take.

Forgiveness can often be thrown around flippantly, but it holds no power unless you genuinely mean what you say.

Is there a situation or someone in your life that you feel is holding you back? Gift yourself the opportunity to take some time to review your life and acknowledge areas where you are still harbouring negativity and reflect upon how forgiveness may also set you free. The true art of forgiveness from your heart and soul is the real pathway out of the pain of your wounds.

As a woman, one way to do this is by connecting to your womb space together with your heart space.

As women, we tend to store much of our pain within the container of our womb, which can inhibit our ability to evolve and may ultimately create disharmony within our physical body.

A client of mine, Anna, was referred to see me for meditation. I knew nothing of Anna's background, only sensing that she was willing to open herself up to healing. She sent me an email the day after our first session to say that she had a profound experience at the circle the previous night, that it allowed her to forgive herself and accept the past trauma of her miscarriage, and that she wanted to continue her spiritual journey with me.

When we are ready for forgiveness and receive healing, the doorway opens for us; the key is to step out of our own way and let the divine light pour through us. Miracles occur on many levels when we are willing to surrender and let go.

Aromatherapy Connection

Using essential oils in conjunction with breathwork is a beautiful and transformative way of tuning into the act of forgiveness. Essential oils used with conscious intent allow you to step out of the left thinking side of the brain and being so head based and step into the right feeling side, allowing you to connect to your heart space.

You can aid the process of forgiveness with essential oils, as the scent of the essential oil directly affects the brain via the olfactory system (as discussed in chapter 5).

Allow yourself to relax in a sacred space where you will not be distracted to undertake this breathwork exercise.

Use the following essential oil forgiveness blend in a diffuser.

- 1 drop of sandalwood
- 1 drop of lavender
- 2 drops of melissa
- 2 drops of frankincense

1. Allow yourself to take a few long, deep breaths into the body, through the nose and holding the breath for a

moment at the top of the inhalation, then deeply and fully breathe out through the mouth.

2. First breath: Place the palm of your right hand on your forehead and place your left hand over your womb space. Inhale through the nose, exhale through the mouth.
3. Second breath: Place your right hand over your heart space and continue to hold your left hand over your womb space. Inhale through the nose, exhale through the mouth.
4. Third breath: Place your right hand over the top of your left hand over your womb space. Inhale through the nose, exhale through the mouth.
5. Do another round of breathing in the above manner, only this time on the inhalation; intuitively direct your breath into your womb and release it through the mouth.
6. On the exhalation, note how your body feels, any associated emotion or feeling, and where you may be holding on to stagnant energy needing release.
7. Continue with this sequence of breathwork until you become fully present in the moment.
8. Once you have developed a sense of calm within, continue to meditate with both hands remaining over your womb (inhaling and exhaling with your natural rhythmic flow) and draw your attention to any aspects of forgiveness you are seeking within.

To gain the most out of this exercise, you must get out of your thinking brain and out of your head and closer to your heart and soul. You may find that on the exhalation, as you deepen your awareness to energetic holding within the body you let out a deep "haaaaa" sound, follow your intuitive flow in this regard.

Quite often, the most incredible healing happens between the breaths, so don't shy away from holding your breath for a moment or two at the top of your inhalation and then really letting go entirely on the exhalation. Bringing your awareness to the space between each breath is a powerful act of intention setting, particularly focusing on the intention to forgive.

Forgiveness Spritz

Create an essential oil spray using the essential oil blend below as a ritual toward letting go of past wounds and hurt from others (or self) and moving closer to love through forgiveness.

In a 200ml spritz bottle, add 150 mls of purified water, then add the following essential oil blend and add a small amount of witch hazel to the blend.

- 10 drops of sandalwood
- 10 drops of lavender
- 8 drops of melissa
- 12 drops of frankincense
- 2 teaspoons of witch hazel

Utilise this spritz as a personal means of setting an intention toward forgiveness before meditation and breathwork.

I have selected the above blend for the following reasons:
- Sandalwood has a sense of serenity about it, helping you to be in charge of your emotions.
- Lavender being the 'mother' of essential oils helps care for your physical and emotional aspects (just as a mother would nurture and take care of an infant).
- Melissa helps to promote intuition and strengthens the wisdom of the heart.

- Frankincense helps to still the mind while in meditation, helping to cut ties with the past and any emotional holding patterns inhibiting your personal growth.

Crystal Connection

Pink, Green or Watermelon Tourmaline are wonderful stones to work with alongside forgiveness.

Green tourmaline helps to create forgiveness and understanding while also allowing you to bring balance and harmony to the heart chakra. In turn, this will enable the healing of old wounds.

Pink tourmaline allows the heart to fully open and let healing in. It also helps you to let go of emotions of blame or guilt, allowing you to sit in a place of deep forgiveness.

Watermelon tourmaline is an amplifier of the two crystals mentioned above and helps to bring compassion to an even deeper level.

Use these crystals in meditation for added benefits of going deeper within. Hold your crystal within one of your hands or lay down and place over your heart chakra (as the heart chakra governs our ability to give and receive love while also bringing acceptance to ourselves and others).

Goddess Connection

Kuan Yin (also Guan Yin or Kwan Yin) is one of the first goddesses that comes to my mind when I think about the concept of forgiveness and bringing a sense of compassion. She is a Chinese Goddess known as the Goddess of Mercy. Kuan Yin is also a Bodhisattva, an *enlightened one* in that she chose not to reach Nirvana to help those of us on the earth plane. Some Chinese legends state that Kuan Yin was the daughter of an evil ruler and that the plague struck her father blind. To heal his eyesight, she gave him the gift of her own eyesight in his place. Her father was stunned by her selfless act, and she was made whole again. Legend would also have her wish to become a Buddhist nun, which was against her father's wishes. When she refused to get married and devote her life to marriage, she was killed and sent to the underworld, only to be returned to life by the Buddha, as the Gods of the underworld didn't like how her essence of purity was turning their world into a paradise.

When her father lost his eyesight, as she so selflessly restored his sight through her own sacrifice, it taught us that two wrongs do not make a right. Instead, we can bear witness to bringing a sense of compassion into our world when someone is struggling or in pain, even if they have wronged us in the past. We each have lessons to learn, and holding compassion, forgiveness and empathy toward another is one of the greatest gifts we may give.

Forgiveness Ritual:
Incorporate the powerful burning bowl ceremony discussed in chapter 7 with the art of burning the written word.

Write a letter to the person you wish to forgive (and perhaps more importantly to yourself). With the burning of the paper into the flames, transformation occurs miraculously for the greater good of all concerned.

Affirmation

"I release the heavy burdens of my past and restore freedom, love and joy within me."

Seed #9:

Acknowledge where you are in your journey of forgiveness and bring acceptance to the stage you are currently in. Holding the intention to bring forgiveness will open doorways toward inner peace and eventually set you free.

One of the most significant critical points in forgiveness is to get out of your head and into your heart space and remember that at our core essence every person is made of pure divine light, just as we are.

CHAPTER 10

The Spirit Guide Connection

Sitting on a lonely, cold bench in Delhi airport, I was a lost woman—a broken and shattered piece of my former self. I sat there quietly, reflecting on the traumatic events that had occurred in the previous days. Little did I realise at the time that it was this inner wound that would eventually assist in the widening of my heart, allowing my soul to further blossom into the courageous woman I am today.

Allow me to walk you through these events so vividly engraved in my heart forever.

It was December 2015. I was travelling with my husband and seven-year-old daughter through India's vibrant, colourful landscape. We were in Agra around the time of my near-death experience, the home of the iconic and much-revered Taj Mahal. It's an icon of devotional love commissioned by emperor Shah Jahan in 1632 to honour his favourite wife, who died while giving birth to their fourteenth child. While staying here in Agra, I experienced a prophetic dream that would change my life forever. I dreamt that something traumatic would happen to me in the days ahead, an event that could potentially be fatal or cause me to suffer physically and alter the trajectory of my life.

The following evening, I became gravely ill, suffering from severe food poisoning. I became weak and listless. During the early morning hours, I had an accident in the hotel bathroom, enduring severe trauma to my head. In my weakened state, I suddenly became dizzy and lightheaded while using the amenities. Then the right side of my head, cheekbone, and teeth smashed against a hard marble pillar next to me, and my limp body fell with a solid thud on the cold tiled floor beneath me.

In the fleeting moments before this accident occurred, I remember feeling dizzy, and the little voice in my head said, "Oh my goodness, my dream from last night, it's happening." At that moment, I knew that there were two paths I could take, one of which I would never return from. One of these paths would lead to severe head trauma and pain and the suffering of physical injuries. In contrast, the other path was more tragic, leading toward death.

Between hitting my head and returning to consciousness, I ventured into a space that was not of this world. It was a space filled with immense light, love, and familiarity, yet simultaneously unknown. I was met by my deceased loved ones, my beloved deceased pets, and people I'd never met but seemed to know me so well. I felt the presence of angels and other light beings who all seemed to welcome me *home*. During the experience, I felt that my senses were heightened and that I could see and feel things beyond my waking awareness. Everything was much more vivid, brighter, colourful, and charismatic. Everything had a clearer image, sharp to the eye, and every detail was enhanced beyond comprehension.

It is the warmest light you could ever imagine seeing. So bright, and yet it doesn't hurt your eyes; it just makes you feel safe and comforted. The colours are vivid and seem like a kaleidoscope of swirling colours in the most amazing hues imaginable. Mixed in with these lights are loved ones from this lifetime welcoming you into their light, and there are faces of people you do not recognise, yet you feel an instant connection to them. It's a feeling that they know you so well. There are the gorgeous pets we have lost in this lifetime, so happy to be reunited.

As a child, I grew up with many pets, especially dogs. I recall seeing my Labradors with their happy, wagging tails and soulful, loving eyes. There are other light beings not of the human form, but they are so welcoming also. There are angels and other spirit guides. It's a true symphony of love and a huge celebration—a homecoming. The depth of love you feel on the other side is like nothing imaginable here on earth. Think of the person you love most in your life, whether they are living or deceased. When you expand this love, it does not even begin to come anywhere near the depth of love waiting for us all on the other side.

To call it unconditional love doesn't do it justice. It is love in its purest, finest, most exquisite form. This love emanates from the support crew that is our spirit guides. Our role while we are travellers on Mother Earth is to extend this feeling of love to those around us and, in a deeper sense, with the essence of who we are within. Every day, we all have the opportunity to rise above our inner wounds and step forward into a life of courageous beauty.

It felt like time went still, and I was floating and drifting between one world and the next. It was like a tug-of-war whether I'd stay or go.

One person that greeted me in this beautiful place of light was the much-loved son I lost through a miscarriage eight years earlier. He held my hand, looked lovingly into my eyes, and heartfully said, "Mummy, I love you, but it's not your time;

you have to go back." I cannot begin to tell you how much these words pained me. To be united with someone I'd never met in the physical world, yet carried within my womb and loved so deeply from conception. Although I never officially knew the sex of our baby, it was an inner knowing that our baby was, in fact, a boy. I also remember conversing with my grandparents and hearing them say how proud they were of me, how much they loved me and that they had been taking such good care of my little boy, who lovingly watches over me all the time, the little boy I'd only ever seen before in spiritual visitations from time to time in meditation.

I was in a state of absolute bliss. It was an overwhelming feeling of peace and love. It was almost euphoric. I was so happy to see those I loved and to feel embraced by the warmth of love that emanated around me. However, I felt immense sadness when I was told it was time to return. I desperately wanted to stay in the warmth of that place where there was seemingly only pure love. This place had no pain or heartache, simply love and complete safety. It felt like we were all one in that space, and I wanted in to this feeling of infinite bliss. Everyone and everything were interconnected, a knowing that we are all a part of the greater whole.

It was overwhelming to be reunited with so many people I cared deeply about in this lifetime and feel their loving presence. To immerse myself in a place where such comfort, joy, love, hope and sense of belonging was, and then to be pulled back with lightning speed to the current day with a sudden thud and jolt of present reality—not to mention the blood, broken teeth and pain of physical injuries and emotional turmoil. It was almost unbearable.

During this dark night of the soul experience, I learned the depth and true meaning of love and the ability to find strength and courage despite the heartache of pain and suffering. Love truly is all that matters. In our essence we are love. It simply feels like here on the earth plane, many of us forget this fact, leading to further pain and suffering as living beings.

One of the most testing and challenging times of my life was endured in India, and yet at the same time, it was one of the most beautiful, heart-opening, loving and inspiring experiences. Life is all about duality, the light and the shadow. We cannot have one without the other and experience pure bliss without equally experiencing the opposite end of the spectrum in some form.

In those fleeting moments I connected to the other side, I was gifted great insight to return to the earth plane. I admit that it has taken me years to fully embrace these gifts as I was overwhelmed and afraid to open the doorway to reveal the truth of what I discovered. It is still a work in progress. Many of you reading this will no doubt understand the concept of the onion layers and how we continue to peel back the layers, revealing who we are at our core, as we rise throughout each level of our existence and work toward healing our inner pain. To reveal the truth of who I am at my core essence and to live and breathe this truth is a daily devotion. This is a truth that many of us fear, and this same truth is the one key element that can set us free to be what we were each incarnated here on earth to embody.

Connecting to the baby I miscarried was a significant part of my experience. The fact that my little boy stopped me from going any further across the veil, given that I still had work to do here on earth, is crucial to my personal mission.

Throughout my two decades in the wellness industry, I often speak about coming from the place of the scar and not the wound. We realise how far we have progressed on the healing journey when we can come from the scar. Through my self-healing journey and writing, I discovered that to heal the wounds left by my experience in India; I had to come face to face with this traumatic time of my life and welcome the wisdom I received with a grateful heart. Only when light is poured upon the shadow of death (in the sense of surrendering to all that no longer serves us) can you truly free yourself from suffering and awaken from the ashes.

I feel a sense of strength knowing that now is the time for me to commence the unveiling of this inner wisdom. The lessons I learned on the other side are submerged within my soul, and divine timing will fully reveal how I can access this wisdom in this lifetime. The wisdom I gained through this passage of time and space in the chamber of death, and now share with women such as yourself, allows for further healing of humankind and in turn, Mother Earth. Like myself, you too can heal from your own unresolved pain. Allow me to help you access this healing by being open to receiving your loving guidance from within.

To understand that despite any heartache, pain and suffering throughout life, we can rise stronger than our inner wounds. This wisdom enables me to share the strength, courage and support from those in the spirit world to assist us through life's challenges. It also serves as a reminder that we are never truly alone on this journey. Those in the realm of spirit are here by our side, lovingly guiding us and supporting us along our path.

I came to realise over the years that if I am to help those around me in whatever way God (or my higher self) wants me to, then I am to face fear head-on, to stare into the reflection of the eyes of my soul and ask the tough questions of myself. What is it that I discovered in the tunnel of time? What is my greater purpose here on earth? Why was I sent back to the physical plane, which can often be filled with intense fear, pain, anger, hurt, frustration, and all the challenges of living a human existence? Why was I sent back instead of living in the blissful state of pure love and light that seemingly appears on the other side?

When I allowed myself to embrace the inner wounds and awaken the core essence of my soul, I discovered my purpose and what I was brought back here to do. A significant part of my soul contract is to share the gift of empowering women to connect to their womb space as a source of healing and creativity. It is also to help them see and believe in their own radiance. It is time that all women are seen, heard, felt and known for their gifts to share with the world. The world is no longer about you and me; it is about *us* and how we may each impact one another in a positive light, to stand tall and proud of being mortals on this earth at this sacred time on the planet.

When the doctor was called to my hotel room after my accident, he suggested I travel home to Australia to deal with my injuries. I felt that the remainder of our trip was significant in my life journey, and so chose to bear the pain so that these lands could help with the emotional healing of my experience, particularly in Varanasi.

The days following my accident in India were all a bit of a blur. I spent many a moment gazing into the Holy River Ganges (the most sacred river in India). Pilgrims (particularly Hindus) would gravitate in droves to India's holiest river, where devotees would come to bathe and wash away their sins. It was here, immersed in the eclectic sounds of life around me and the streams of vivid colours of Indian clothing being washed along the ghats, that I contemplated the intensity of the traumatic event that had just happened to me. The waters of Mother Ganga swallowed my tears of internal sadness, helping me wash away my pain so that I could continue living a life I wasn't sure I wanted to be in.

Sitting on a small wooden boat amid these holy waters, my husband, together with our daughter, sat while I meditated at the bow of the boat, watching the sunrise as the hope of another day unfolded before us.

I desperately wanted these holy waters to wash away my tears, purify my soul, and make me feel whole again. I felt in shock, wondering why it all happened and why I was pulled back to living in human form in what can often be the harsh reality of our modern world.

It took me years to come to terms with being back on earth. I felt torn between those I love here on earth and those that I still love on the other side, and the depth of unconditional love emanating from the other side that pulls at me like a magnet wanting more.

That time of my life was a double-edged sword. On the one hand, I witnessed the vivid colours, the intense warmth, the place where pain is non-existent, and love is in its purest form, a love that cannot be fully expressed or felt on the earth plane. Then, on the other hand, upon my return, I felt guilt, sadness and heartache for returning to a world with people I loved and yet a longing to return to the light. I felt torn between present day existence and my beautiful life and a yearning to return to what felt like the *real home* in a realm a mere heartbeat away.

I felt that it was not my choice to come back to earth. I wasn't given a preference to decide if I wanted to have this realm or the next. My higher self was in charge. My destiny would have me return to this earthly life, for it is here that my greatest mission is to be accomplished, and there are no exceptions.

The waters of the Ganges are believed to wash away sins and purify the soul. This is precisely how it felt for me as I drifted on the waters in the wooden boat, placing offerings of marigolds and candles into the waters at sunrise and sunset, listening to the sounds of pilgrims bathing on the ghats in Varanasi and witnessing multiple cremations along the banks and watching the smoke gently rise into the air. The solitude, the silence, and the ability to breathe life again filled my soul with the strength to continue and know that, despite any heartache and pain from recent trauma, I was gifted the opportunity to continue my journey and live out my purpose at this particular time on earth. I was given a second chance in life, a gift of wiping the slate clean and having the waters of the Ganges renew my spirit so I may step up and fully reclaim my role.

My experience taught me that if you have a dream, allow yourself the ability to follow through and pursue it. Before India, I knew I wanted to reach out and help people heal in ways far greater than I previously did through massage and energy healing alone. I wanted to step more into the coaching arena, and I needed to alter how I worked with clients, which also meant further study. My studies took me abroad to the United States of America, where I left behind my husband and daughter for a short time while I pursued my career, training as a Soul Coaching® Practitioner, and then later again to study aspects of the Goddess at Denise Linn's *Red Lotus Mystery School*. I also knew deep inside that I had a book that needed to be written, a calling that had been within me all my life. I felt this more intensely after my near-death experience. We all are born to shine, and we all have gifts, talents and abilities just waiting to be reclaimed. Still, first we must believe in ourselves and hold the courage to make our dreams a reality.

You would not be here right now, in our living existence, if you were not meant to actively play your part in some way. Sometime in your life, you've chosen to play it small. You've decided not to speak up for fear of judgement.

We are not put on this earth plane to play a smaller version of ourselves. Spirit and the Creator within all things want us to shine equally, be at our brightest, and share our greatness with the world. When one person shines their light, we pave the way for our sisters and brothers to do the same.

My near-death experience taught me many things, one of which is the power of love for the physical world here on the earth plane (especially for the people in our lives that we hold most dear), for our loved ones who reside in the spiritual realm, and for the self-love that we are constantly working on within. Life can be taken from us at any moment, and our time here is precious. As previously mentioned earlier in this book, while I do believe we do not necessarily have to suffer to grow, my experience capturing the essence of pure unconditional love and witnessing first-hand the intensity that our ancestors, guides and other light beings hold for us has given me greater depth to my authentic teachings, which I am here to share into the world.

India will forever hold a special place in my heart, but it is somewhat of a double-edged sword—love and beauty mixed with heartache and pain. Life is all about duality, the light and the shadow; one cannot exist without the other. Both are equally powerful and teach us different aspects for us to learn, grow and evolve.

To own all the parts of you, it's time to embrace your light and bring acceptance to your shadow self. I'm here to help you do just that. Every day, we are given moments to shine our light to react and respond in ways that raise our vibration. Some days life may be harder to deal with, and some days are more manageable. All we can ever ask of ourselves is to show up and be uniquely ourselves, inner wounds and all. Through our wounds, we transform our lessons into pearls of wisdom.

Look back on your past hurts and witness the growth these lessons gifted you. As difficult as it may be, there is always something to be grateful for. Gather your journal, find a comfortable place where you won't be interrupted, and spend time sifting through your past wounds and finding the hidden jewels of wisdom from these lessons.

We have many spirit guides who assist us on our journey in this life, and at least one full time spirit guide with us 24/7 from birth until death. Some of our guides come in for specific periods, and others come and go as required by us.

Connecting with your personal spirit guides can assist you in receiving guidance, help, clarity and insight along your path. It can also enhance your spiritual journey in general.

Our spirit helpers connect with us in many ways. When we are open to receiving their loving guidance, our connection deepens, as do the signs, symbols and synchronicities.

Some signs may be:

- Blown light bulbs – like electricity, spirits are a form of energy working at a high vibration. If there are flickering lights in the house, or if your television, computer or other electrical appliances are disturbed, it could be that your spirit guides want to get your attention.
- Songs on the radio – if suddenly a song comes on the radio that reminds you of a loved one in spirit, it may be that they are alongside you, wanting you to receive a message.
- Dreams – this is a common way our spirit guides like to connect with us, as it's when we are most relaxed and open to receive.

One of the ways that spirit likes to connect with me is through feathers, particularly small white feathers. When I see these cross my path in random or unusual places, I always feel an instant connection to my loved ones in Heaven. If it's a small feather, I know that my little boy in Heaven is shining down even more brightly upon me, encouraging me on my path.

There are so many ways we may receive signs. Start to bring your conscious awareness to things that are a little out of the ordinary and pause at that moment to consider if a spirit helper is trying to get a message to you and exactly what that message may be.

Some other ways we may receive signs are things like random coins that may appear on the ground, car number plates that stand out to us for seemingly no reason, seeing numbers on a clock such as 11:11, or seeing specific numbers repeatedly. Nature is another beautiful way of receiving messages from the realm of spirit. You will experience times when you know you have received something special, such as certain cloud formations or certain animals that may cross your path that is out of the ordinary.

Our spirit guides make themselves known in various ways, such as hearing little buzzing noises in our ear(s), seeing flashes of light, or letting you physically feel their presence nearby.

I will now share an exercise enabling you to deepen your intuition, expanding upon your feminine powers of rich inner knowing.

Soulful Exercise

I welcome you to further your connection to those in the realm of spirit, who are only too happy to assist you along your path. Spirit is there to help us; all we need to do is be open to receiving and trusting their loving guidance. Asking for help from our spirit guides can allow us to release some of the burdens we carry with our inner wounds. For we are never truly alone in life.

Find a space where you will not be distracted and create sacred space for yourself. Create an ambience by lighting a candle (the flame representing our connection to spirit through the element of fire), burn incense or have essential oils (refer to the aromatherapy section at the end of this chapter) in a diffuser to arouse the senses. Play some gentle background relaxation music or listen to the sounds of nature outside to help you unwind. Creating an ambience enables you to switch off from pure thinking mode and into the intuitive side of feeling. Close your eyes and allow yourself time to deeply connect with your breath and notice how your body feels. Use your imagination to surround yourself with beautiful white light around your physical body and that of your auric field (the subtle body surrounding your physical self), knowing that you are safe to go within.

Breathing deeply and fully, filling your lungs with air, breathing into your belly, your chest and up to your collarbone, and then letting all the air out of your body in reverse, collarbone, chest and belly. Allow each breath to take you deeper into that quiet place. Continue this breathing, allowing your abdomen to expand like a balloon and then contract. As you relax more and more, allow yourself to feel safe and fully supported.

Call in your spirit helpers by inviting them with the following invocation:

"As I deepen my breath, I deepen my connection to the realm of spirit and invite those who are of the light and for my highest good, to lovingly assist me today. I easily and effortlessly receive the messages my soul needs to hear. I call forward my spirit helpers and give thanks for their loving guidance."

Allow yourself time to connect within. Place your hands over your heart or your womb space to deepen your connection to your physical body and allow yourself to get out of your thinking and analytical mind and move deeper into your heart space.

Be still, open your heart, and all you need do is ask. Spirit shall present itself to you in a multitude of ways, for example, through visions in your spiritual sight (clairvoyance), through physical or emotional feelings (clairsentience), things you hear in your mind or with physical ears (clairaudience), through smells (such as tobacco from a deceased loved one who previously smoked) which are not present in the physical realm (clairalience) and other ways of getting your attention.

Each time you consciously connect to your spirit helpers, power and awareness build within you. Developing our intuition and assistance from the spirit realm is much like going to the gym to build our muscle strength; the more we use it, the stronger and healthier we become. Our spirit helpers are lovingly walking beside us in every moment to help bring us strength, courage, healing and inner wisdom.

I recall around the one year anniversary of my grandmother's death, that my mother and I went to the place where her ashes were scattered down by the ocean. As the sun was setting on this beautiful spring evening, a bird caught my attention and I photographed it with the sun setting in the backdrop and the beautiful cloud formations above. I had a strong intuitive urge to take that photograph and felt that there would be something special to see later on. When we got home, I looked at the photo, and an image of my grandmother's face was within the cloud formation! My mother and I saw it instantly, and it was most definitely a sign from my grandmother in the spirit realm speaking to us and through us. I would have missed this beautiful opportunity if I didn't follow my intuition, not only by taking the photo but in the knowingness (claircognisance) that there was something special to see in the image.

As you deepen your daily devotional connection to the realm of spirit together with watching for signs, your intuition builds, and you allow yourself to trust that you are never alone. Be sure to thank your guides regularly for their assistance along your path. A simple "thank you" said internally is enough to show your gratitude for their help. Gratitude for all in your life goes a long way, and this also extends to your spirit guide helpers. Remember that those in the realm of spirit—be it deceased loved ones, angels, ascended masters, goddess energies, animal totems, fairies, elementals or other light beings—are only a request away and are readily available to help you.

In the following pages, I bring you ways to enhance further your ability to connect to the realm of spirit to help you understand the whispers of your soul.

Aromatherapy Connection

Using essential oils to enhance your connection to spirit is a valuable and powerful tool.

Frankincense would have to be my ultimate "go-to" as an oil to enhance spiritual connection. It can assist you in helping to open your third eye (home of your intuition), while also protecting and shielding your energy. It is often referred to as the *king of oils*.

One of the powerful aspects of aromatherapy is the ability to ignite memories. Something that has always enchanted and brought me joy in a church is when the resin of frankincense (alongside benzoin and myrrh) would waft through the air in a thurible incense burner. It brings back ancient past life memories hidden deep within me. Sound is another way in which to invoke memories within. Being in various churches across the globe, ones that have Gregorian chanting, while also immersing myself within the scent of frankincense, has constantly enriched my soul.

I recall visiting the Black Madonna at Our Lady of Montserrat in Spain, listening to the sounds of Gregorian chants among the aromatic scents, and having it transport me to feelings of times gone by in prior lifetimes. Scholars have said that the Black Madonna may represent the archetypal Earth Mother, the ancient eternal power of the divine feminine.

There are many theories about the background of the Black Madonna and what she represents. As mentioned above, some say that she is an ancient Earth Goddess converted to Christianity (if you were to think of fertile soil, the richer and more black the soil is, the more suitable it is for agriculture).

Other theories suggest that the Virgin Mary statues have turned black in colour due to deterioration over the years or from the smoke of votive candles continuously burning. Perhaps you have your own theory or may leave it with no explanation necessary, just another of life's beautiful mysteries of the divine feminine.

Some other suggested oils to use in an oil burner or diffuser to assist with your spiritual connection are:

- Lavender – a relaxing aroma distilled from her soft purple flowers and leaves. It is a calming oil that also helps raise your vibration, taking your spiritual journey to the next level.
- Palo Santo – known as *holy wood*, has a rich and sweet aroma (similar in some ways to licorice), helping to energetically cleanse your space while also bringing a sense of calm.
- Sandalwood – a rich, woody scent that helps to ground your emotions and ease anxiety while connecting you to divine universal wisdom, merging you with Heaven and Earth.

Crystal Connection

I encourage you to enhance your connection to the spirit realm through crystals. One crystal I love to use personally—particularly to connect me to the angelic realm—is that of angelite. It is a blissful shade of lilac blue and holds a very gentle yet powerful energy. It is a beautiful stone that may assist you in speaking your truth and opens the pathway to spiritual inspiration. It particularly helps with our connection to our angelic guides.

Hold this stone in meditation or place it upon the body where you feel intuitively guided, helping to balance the physical body with the etheric realms.

Some other crystal suggestions to help in your connection to your spirit guides are:

- Amazonite – a stone of communication and truth, it helps to calm an overactive mind and make space for clarity to be found.
- Green aventurine – a comforting stone for the heart, helping to renew optimism for life and all that we want to acquire in the world.
- Jade – this stone signifies wisdom and connection to who you really are while increasing love and nurturing of self.
- Turquoise – a protective stone to aid in communication with the physical and spiritual world, enhancing intuition. It helps to release stagnant energy and light the path toward balanced self-expression and wisdom.

Over time, as you work with crystals more, you will find crystals that resonate specifically with you and what you need. The above crystals mentioned are only suggestions, but there are many more. Use your intuition and let that be your internal guide.

Goddess Connection

Throughout life as a woman, there are times when we may wish to call upon certain spirit helpers to assist us throughout our life's journey even more. The following are some beautiful Goddess energies that will help you throughout your life as a glorious woman.

Maiden

The phase of a woman's life representing new beginnings, spring time, freedom, rebirth, adventure and desire.

Goddess Examples:

- Brigid: stoking the flames of fertility in the sense of all that you wish to birth in the world.

- Danu: accessing the power of water (like the waters held within the sacred chalice of your womb) to understand that you are in the process of all that you are becoming.
- Ostara (also known as Eostre): drawing upon your fertility and the ripeness within to start implementing your creative ideas.
- Persephone: cultivating your inner growth and happiness and the wisdom found in being in a state of open-hearted learning.

Mother

It is important to remember that to embody the *mother* energy, you do not necessarily have to be a physical mother. This is the energy used to birth creations in this world. It represents the time of summer and the ability to find the balance of caring for your own needs whilst also nurturing the needs of others.

Goddess Examples:

- Aine: inspires and encourages passion within to use your powers for creativity and healing and to step outside your comfort zone.
- Demeter: to teach you about the power of harvesting and producing within and understanding the balance of sharing this harvest with others.
- Freya: invoking happiness toward the love of self, in cultivating relationships and the gift of acceptance.
- Isis: using your wound wisdom to strengthen and manifest change by reclaiming a healthier version of yourself.

Maga

This is the pre-menstrual phase of a woman's life when women start to release fears of survival, self-acceptance and self-love. It is also the time of autumn.

Goddess Examples:

- Frigg: assisting you with entering your intuitive side (particularly that of clairvoyance) while still keeping this wisdom a little closer to your chest before you are ready to have this energy birthed into the world for all to see.
- Hestia: helping you cultivate the home within yourself to provide protection and warmth in sustaining life.
- Pachamama: assisting you with the nourishment you need to survive and be abundant in all areas of your life.
- Prithvi: allowing you to sustain your life here on earth through creativity and transformation.

Crone

This represents the wise woman within. She represents maturity, wisdom, experience, knowledge, knowing, understanding and the time of winter.

Goddess Examples:

- Cailleach: helping you understand the storms of life during your darker times.
- Cerridwen: assisting you to understand aspects of death giving rise to rebirth and reaching your full potential.
- Hecate: helping you understand the crossroads of life and what is required of you to move forward.
- Lilith: helping you with your self-worth and self-respect and your ability to stand up for what you believe in with absolute courage and empowered independence.

It is important to note that sometimes there is an overlap with Goddess qualities that may weave between the archetypes. Trust which Goddess comes forward when working with the differing phases of your life as a woman. The Goddess aligned with your energies and specific needs will be called forth accordingly, through divine guidance.

A spirit guide of mine who has been with me all my life is that of Mother Mary. It has taken the womanly phase of motherhood for me to deepen my connection with her. Growing up as a child, I was never raised in a religious family environment, although we had our beliefs. Since my marriage, I have been affiliated with the Catholic faith. I cherish my connection to Mother Mary, despite not being Catholic myself. I have my own special connection to her in my own way. We each have the freedom to follow our chosen belief system regarding religious faith, which resonates with the individual. My connection to Mother Mary is a particularly strong one and was solidified even more so while visiting sacred sites around the world that have a special connection to her.

During the most challenging times throughout my life, such as the miscarriage I endured, I have often felt her presence near me. She has been right at my side when I have needed her loving presence (in times of great sadness and grief). I have even felt her warm, comforting embrace on occasion, the embrace a mother would give to comfort a child in distress. Mother Mary is often referred to as the *mother of mothers*, and I know that I only need to call her, and she will answer with her caring and loving guidance.

Mother Mary is known for her compassion, nurturing spirit, and protection. She offers great comfort and emotional support for those in need. She has a particular devotion to helping the upbringing of children and their welfare.

I recall her loving presence while travelling in Lourdes, France, many years ago. This was an insightful time spent connecting with her beautiful motherly energy. Lighting candles of intention at the grotto within the Sanctuary of Our Lady of Lourdes is a particularly fond memory. So too, was spending quiet time reflecting within the Basilica of Our Lady of Lourdes (refer to chapter 11 for further reflection on the healing power of the water energy at Lourdes). I have connected with Mother Mary's energies in many other places around the world, particularly at Marian apparition sites (where supernatural appearances have been reported). My connections to Mother Mary and Marian apparition sites beyond Lourdes, France, have been far and wide, including Fatima in Portugal, Montserrat in Spain and Siluva in Lithuania. The world is rich and full of a tapestry of connections to this beautiful guide, who we may each connect with easily and effortlessly whenever we call her name.

We can connect to our spirit guides in many ways, and evoking is one way we may bring direct intention to their loving guidance. Much like we have called upon specific Goddess archetypes in other chapters by inwardly calling their name and asking for their support. We can do the same with our loved ones in the spirit world or other guides with whom we begin to form a connection with over time.

When you are feeling discouraged and alone, seek further guidance from your spiritual allies, and allow yourself to connect through meditation by calling them forward, similarly to the way I do with Mother Mary as my guide. The overarching message here is that we all need to know that our guides support us throughout our daily adventures and that we are never alone.

I like to consider myself open spiritually to guidance that I need throughout my life from the spirit realm as a whole. By being open, I broaden my awareness that there are many religious faiths and all deserve to be treated with respect. We can gain great insight into ourselves when we sit in a place of non-judgment. While accepting that we may not always know the answers to all of life's questions, we can be a clear channel for allowing daily messages from our guides to pour through.

It has been said that Mother Mary had been trained by Eastern Sages in meditation for countless lifetimes in order to prepare her womb to be the purified vessel for Jesus by light conception. I believe I allowed Mother Mary to step forward more into my awareness once I became a mother. When I had my miscarriage, she was with me; throughout my second pregnancy, I felt her around me; during the child-rearing of my daughter, I know she supports me. Sometimes through life, we can forget that, despite being adults, we still need that nurturing support around us that a mother may give. Mother Mary offers me this nurturing and comforting love, and my own physical mother, with whom I have a strong bond in this lifetime.

We as women, can connect with our womb as a source of healing and creativity. While we may not pursue the same miraculous abilities that Mother Mary did, we each have the miraculous ability to see, feel and know that our womb space is indeed sacred, and we should treat it as such. Mother Mary understood the holiness of the womb. Particularly during pregnancy, we as women can shine a light on the unborn child growing within us.

We can also do the same for the other seeds of creation we wish to bring forth into this world. Every woman is the mother of creative projects, ideas and dreams. To focus on these particular seeds of creation, we may access the space of our womb in meditation. One specific way is to visualise an orange ball of liquid light (orange being the colour of the sacral chakra), filling your womb with love and creative energy.

If you have a particular project that you are working on *birthing* into the world, you then bring your awareness to this project and imagine seeds being planted within your womb (much like the conception of a baby) and beginning to sprout, grow leaves and strengthen within you. You are setting and planting the seeds of intention; every creative endeavour starts within our womb space and cultivates with time until it is ready to enter the world alongside us. When we continue to nurture, nourish and bring action toward fostering our creations, they will be birthed into our world in time.

Affirmation

Use the affirmation below to help aid your connection to your spirit guide helpers.

"I am open to receiving the support and loving guidance from those in the realm of spirit."

Seed #10

Throughout our time on Mother Earth, we are never alone; our spirit helpers are our companions, helping to guide, nurture and love us as we navigate the waters of our world. As we connect more intimately with our spirit guides, we discover a unique bond that never breaks. This bond strengthens the more we allow their loving support within our lives.

CHAPTER 11

Healing with Nature

Basking in the hot arid summer's sunshine walking the base of Uluru, I heard the ancients (in the realm of spirit) talking to me as I connected deep within myself to listen to the voice of the land. With beads of sweat slowly dripping down the side of my temples, wiping my brow from the perspiration, I listened intuitively for the words and wisdom this sacred land had to share with me. It was the second time I'd travelled to the rich red centre of Australia, only this time around, my level of conscious awareness had increased tenfold from the previous visit, and this time I was ready to intently hear what the rhythm of the earth wanted to share with me. While seated nearby the rock itself and channelling through meditation, I was gifted a spirit name during my time in Uluru. My name, *Mulanjurrah* pronounced "Mool-un-ja-rah" when I hear it said through soul consciousness, is a blend of indigenous cultures from all over the world that are bound together to help me on my journey forward.

Are you aware of the origins of your name and how you came to be known? Our names hold deep resonance and help identify your soul energy. Some cultures still emphasise the founding of a child's name when born. In our Western culture, we tend not to think so much about what goes into what we are named, yet it still holds great power regardless. Often as we journey further along our spiritual path, we may place more consideration upon the names in which we are gifted as children and whether or not we choose to use the full expression of our name or if we shorten it and how the names we use for ourselves resonate within.

While travelling in Uluru, I did not go there in search of my "spiritual name", but it was an extra special birthday gift at the time. This name to me has always felt like the weaving of all of my ancient cultural threads and experiences as a fusion of my soul remembrance. Finding your spiritual name may be something you may choose to think about. You may ask your guides to assist you in meditation or within your dream state and have pen and paper ready to write down what you may hear.

Tuning into the natural world around you is a beautiful key for discovering more of who you are and what gifts, talents and abilities you have that are ready to be explored further and used.

When women want to look at ways in which they may start the healing process and obtain the most out of life, they can often look at honing in on only one particular area. For instance, if your career isn't going as well as you would like, you could seize this opportunity to update and enhance your resume in search of your dream job. Then what can happen is that you successfully secure a new job opportunity and find that nothing has changed significantly. It may be a different job, a different workplace, but the same old monotonous feelings on the inside are still prevalent. We can all be guilty of this pattern throughout our life, whether it be our careers, our relationships (e.g. partners who do not treat you respectfully), our finances (e.g. always limited with funds or overspending) etc. When these patterns of behaviour repeat themselves over and over again, it's time to consider starting afresh and looking deeper into the real substance of the re-occurring pattern.

Afterall, the *self* goes where you go, if the patterns of behaviour don't alter, it follows you wherever you go. An area I've witnessed as a coach working with clients is that, too often, people focus all their attention on one particular area instead of viewing themselves as a part of the greater whole. For instance, somebody may be looking at their physical health and placing all their focus here that they omit to look at other areas of their body, such as their mental, emotional and spiritual components. When it comes to healing the body, the mind, and the spirit also deserve equal attention.

When looking at the body as a whole, the notion of looking at nature as a means of healing comes into play. Our mental, emotional, spiritual and physical selves directly correlate to the elements of nature, being that of air, water, fire and earth. When we weave the threads of these aspects of self, we have a more significant opportunity to evolve as a whole.

Since my near-death experience, I have discovered a greater depth of connection to the earth and her elements and how we can access these elements of nature for more remarkable healing and inner harmony.

For almost two decades, I have lived in two homes, one in the city and one along the coast. While I love both houses and they support our family in different ways, our home on the coast gives us the sense of freedom we desire. Time spent here also allows the soul to breathe and return to city life with a reinvigorated spirit and ability to serve the community within our respective careers. Something magical about being alongside the concept of water fills and replenishes our spirit. Aspects of this very book have been written while overlooking the body of water that I am blessed to be able to call home on the stunning Fleurieu Peninsula in South Australia. While for the most part, this book was written (particularly in its latter stages) while sitting nearby the high tree tops of my city home, listening to the rustling of the wind and the sound of birds chirping amongst the striking skyline outside my home studio.

Some time ago, I constructed a medicine wheel (a gathering of stones in a circle representing the four cardinal directions and the aspects of self (mental, emotional, spiritual and physical) based upon Native American traditions next to my home on the coast. This activated medicine wheel keeps me connected to the energy of this land where ever I am.

Spending time in nature can heal us from the inside out. When we immerse ourselves in the beauty of the natural environment around us, we allow ourselves to be like our ancestors. Our ancestors in times gone by would look to nature as a source of wisdom, inspiration and guidance. Whether it was to help tune in and locate where the catch of the day would be or to know when a storm was brewing, it was nature that gifted the answers to the questions they sought. Our ancestors would connect with nature daily for survival; through this connection, they understood the depth of everything in life.

These days we can be so caught up with technology and spend a significant amount of time under artificial lighting that our sense of connection to the natural cycles and rhythms of the world around us can become hazy and disconnected. As women, our cycles are also affected. In times gone by, our ancestors attuned themselves to the moon; sleeping under the stars and moonlight, bleeding on a new moon, often occurred as a collective within the tribal community.

When we allow ourselves to spend time in nature, not only does it replenish our soul, but it will enable us to still the mind and receive messages from the world around us. The clouds, the ocean, the bird life, the animals, the wind in the trees, the rock formations, everything in nature has wisdom to share with us when we slow down and listen.

The source of many of my teachings has come from spending time in nature all over the globe and gathering wisdom from the land, particularly at various sacred sites. This wisdom and knowledge from all that I've ever experienced throughout my world travel sit within me. I am a part of the land, and the land is a part of me, it's a fair exchange of energies between us, just as it can be for you also.

Within each of us, we have a landscape in nature that resonates at a cellular level. For me, it's the element of water. For others, you may find that being out amongst more earthy elements, such as the bush or in the mountains, may resonate with you more. The landscape or scenery is not as relevant as the messages you receive within it and how the land makes you feel. As I just mentioned, I have a deep fondness for the element of water and yet, by being among the rich earthly energies at Uluru I received profound messages from spirit. I was open to receiving and quieting my mind so that nature could speak to and through me. A key aspect of healing through nature is to be still, quiet the mind and listen for the messages from the earth and the universe.

Start to become in tune with nature around you and begin to notice, for instance, when the rain falls around you—instead of viewing it as a nuisance at having to pull out your umbrella, allow yourself to view it as an opportunity to not only cleanse the land but to also clear and cleanse your soul at the same time. It also allows you to witness the direct correlation that the element of water has upon our connection to our emotions and what we as a woman may need to clear and cleanse.

As a woman, the element of water, particularly, weaves its connection to the feminine spirit. The womb itself is like a body of water, a sacred chalice. When we were a foetus in our mother's womb, the womb itself was surrounded by amniotic fluid. When we immerse ourselves in water it replicates the environment within the womb, which is one of the reasons that it can be mighty powerful for women to have water births or to use water as a tool throughout pregnancy.

When coaching clients I love to have them acknowledge the natural world around them and bring this into their everyday life. While it's lovely to observe the beauty around you while on vacation on a tropical island, there need not be only glimpses of a time when you witness this beauty around you. There is beauty, lessons and learning all around us each day, and nature offers us the opportunity to tune in. The key is to slow down and listen. There are messages within the soft, gentle breeze of a warm summer's evening, just as there are messages to receive from the torrential winter rain, the falling leaves of autumn, or the chirping of baby birds in the spring. At one stage during the editorial phase of this book, a wild autumn storm had been building throughout the night. Upon waking, I found fallen tree limbs throughout my local area, including my backyard. It happened to be around the autumnal equinox, so I considered this as Mother Nature's way of allowing winds of change to be felt on many levels. I saw it as a seasonal change and paving the way toward weaving more from light to dark, from summer to autumn. Equally, as nature changes around you, take the opportunity to get curious as to what is being stirred up on a more personal level.

One of the daily rituals I love to do constantly is going out in nature and walking my dog. It gives me the perfect opportunity to witness the elements, notice the clouds, feel the sun's rays on my face and ask the question of myself, "what does my soul want me to know today?". Observing the natural environment gives us so many messages if we only pause long enough to listen.

Nature is cyclical, and so are we. Just like the seasons turn and change, we do this also. By tuning into the natural rhythms of life around us, it enables us to further tune into spirit inside of us and our true nature on a personal and soul level. Start to consciously become aware of the natural world around you and open your eyes and ears to the messages you see, feel and hear with all your senses.

Within my own life, I predominantly follow the Native American four-element system of air, water, fire and earth for my connection to the elements, and it's what I choose to use with my clients. Although I acknowledge there are other elements within different cultures worth exploring if you so desire.

When we understand how to weave these elements within our lives, the mundane tasks or how we observe nature shifts. It shifts so that we acknowledge that within each cycle and season, there are gifts to be received from a source greater than ourselves, and we may learn such depth from the natural world around us.

As individuals, we can also be categorised into these four elements in conjunction with our zodiac birth signs.

Air = Gemini, Libra, Aquarius

Water = Cancer, Scorpio, Pisces

Fire = Aries, Leo, Sagittarius

Earth = Taurus, Virgo, Capricorn

The element of air corresponds to our *mental* aspect, from our thoughts and beliefs and the patterns of behaviour we display. The left "thinking" side of our brain is activated when we use our minds and focus on thought, the analytical side of us as humans. Breath is vital to the element of air—it's the oxygen we breathe daily without even giving it a second thought. There is an exchange between nature and yourself between each and every breath you take. When you breathe in you are receiving a gift of oxygen from the natural world through the trees and plants. In return on the out-breath, you exhale carbon dioxide, which is returned to the trees and plants. When you bring that into form from an elemental point of view, you can think about the wind that blows through the trees—the winds of change around you or you might think about the clouds drifting in the abundant blue sky above. When you think of air you can think about new life, communication and the power of your mind.

Water has the ability to cleanse and purify and allows you to be in the flow of life. The element of water corresponds to the *emotional* aspect of you. It correlates to how you feel and make sense of the world around you. The right "feeling" side of your brain is activated when you notice your emotions and tune into the intuitive part of yourself. Our psychic ability is enhanced by the element of water and accessing our subconscious.

The element of fire corresponds to the *spiritual* aspect of you, and I always love to share with clients that fire can be both transformative and destructive according to how you work with it. It's also about creation itself and rising to give form to new ways of being in your world and your perspective on your challenge at hand.

The element of earth corresponds to your *physical* aspect of self. Allowing you to be grounded, safe and secure with the foundations you set for yourself and your place in the world.

As a woman, we are so intrinsically woven to all of the elements of nature but one that I have previously mentioned that in particular has a distinctly intense resonance personally is the element of water. As humans, we are made up of almost 70% water within our bodies, and it's this factor that I believe we have such a healing resonance with bodies of water around us. From the oceans, the rivers, the lakes and the streams, all of these replicate the water we hold and the water that, as women we hold within the sacred chalice of our womb.

Dr Emoto, a Japanese scientist who discovered that molecules of water are affected by our thoughts, words and feelings, states that the average human body is made up of 70% water. We start life being 99% water, as a foetus. When we are born, we are 90% water, and by the time we reach adulthood, we are down to 70%. We will be about 50% water if and when we die of old age. In other words, throughout our lives, *we exist primarily as water.* You may further investigate the powerful connection of the healing vibrations of water through the wise teachings of Dr Emoto.

Water connects you to your sacral chakra, your intuitive and creative space of your womb. The womb is where life begins in all its forms and where it gives rise to all that you can be through your capacity to embody the Goddess within.

When I had my near-death experience, it was on and beside the waters of the Holy River Ganges that soothed my soul and held me together when all I wanted was to crumble and disintegrate into the earth. I was a mere shell of a human being. It was floating along the Ganges and feeling the purification of these waters, and seeing pilgrims bathing alongside the ghats of Varanasi, that enabled me to witness the flow of life within me, despite my emotional and physical turmoil.

The bodies of water that I have immersed in across the globe have strengthened my spirit and enabled deep learning from nature. The beauty that water can do to revitalise, restore and replenish the soul is immeasurable.

One of the most cherished memories I have that reflects how water affects us on many levels comes from the healing waters in Lourdes, France.

There are so many stories I could share about my travels across the globe, especially ones that have taken me off the beaten path, not knowing exactly why I was called to travel to these locations until much later, simply following my womanly intuition.

It was the Christmas/new year period in 2014 on one particular journey back to France (a country that speaks to me at soul level). As a family, we set off on a pilgrimage toward Lourdes by train, only to have tragedy strike further down the line involving an unfortunate fatal accident. The entire train was offloaded, and all train travellers then went by bus for the remainder of the journey. When we finally arrived in Lourdes it was getting dark, and construction workers were fencing off the grotto at Our Lady of Lourdes. It was apparent that major renovations were happening immediately around this site, and it was being closed to the public. We were naturally disheartened, yet our prayers to enter were answered, as we were thankfully given private access, it seemed like a miracle. We were the last family to enter before the site was shut to all pilgrims.

It was here in Lourdes that I could deeply connect with Our Lady of Lourdes, Mother Mary and the healing waters at the grotto. It was indeed a sight beyond words; the spiritual magnitude of the energy in this location was phenomenal. It is said that Marian water stores all the loving prayers and energy associated with Mother Mary and the angels. If you ever get to visit this sacred place, I highly recommend it.

Visiting this sacred site in the small French town of Lourdes connected me more intimately with Mother Mary, who has always been a powerful guiding influence in my life. This small town is where one of the most famous apparitions of the Blessed Virgin Mary took place in 1858. A young girl named Bernadette Soubirous was out gathering firewood with her sister and friend near a grotto when she saw a vision of a lovely lady. In the words of St Bernadette, "I raised my head and looked towards the grotto. I saw a lady wearing a white dress, a blue girdle and a yellow rose on each foot, the same colour as the chain of her Rosary".

The Lourdes story has Mary appearing to the peasant girl Bernadette 18 times between 11th February 1858 and 16th July 1858. On the ninth apparition, the "miraculous" spring is discovered, but it is at the 17th apparition that "the Lady" reveals to Bernadette who she is. Since that time, pilgrims have visited this shrine in the hope of a cure, to deepen their spiritual lives and also out of sheer curiosity. Many claim to have been cured of illnesses and restoring their health from the healing waters in Lourdes, and many also speak of their spiritual growth for having been in this sacred place. I can attest to the potent energy present here and feel fortunate to have bathed in the healing waters of the grotto there with the assistance of the Catholic nuns, a unique experience I shall never forget.

The Marian water experience was one that I am at a loss to explain except to further believe in miracles fully. Sitting in my hotel, my husband encouraged me to undertake the bathing experience. I was apprehensive about getting naked in front of strangers (albeit Catholic nuns). However, I am forever grateful for my husband's encouragement, and I am proud of myself for being able to put aside my insecurities. I went with my heart wide open to receive.

The Catholic nuns warmly welcomed me at the Baths, and while they did not speak to me in English, they motioned to me to head toward an area with several stalls with curtains around them. Once behind the curtain, I undressed, and an assistant helped me by wrapping me in a blue cape as I awaited my turn to bathe in the healing waters. When it was my turn, the assistant helped me step toward the bath and then replaced the blue cape with a thin white one dipped into the tub. The nun then motioned me toward the steps leading into the bath while having two assistants, one on either side, as

I submerged my entire body (apart from my head) into what felt like phenomenal healing water, while taking a moment to contemplate and connect with the energies of Mother Mary and the presence of God. Upon exiting the bath, it was pretty unbelievable how fast my body could dry off. One moment I was fully immersed in water; the next, I was completely dry! It all adds to the mystery and majesty of this sacred and holy place.

How anyone can bathe, be submerged in water, and come out dry is truly a miracle, and yet, having experienced this for myself, I can vouch for the truth and what a unique experience it indeed is. Immersion within these waters has ceased since the COVID-19 pandemic, with a *water gesture* as an alternative with pilgrims bathing their faces, hands and forearms using the spring water. Hopefully, the immersion bathing experience will eventually return, as it truly needs to be felt to be understood completely.

I shall never forget this bathing experience. I brought some of the water from the healing springs home to Australia. The Lourdes water I gathered at the site has since been used to make special essential oil spritzers, and the energy of these spritzers are powerful. I also regularly use the collected holy water on altars at home, and during the women's circles I facilitate. This water energy purifies the heart, womb and soul.

It was winter when I visited this shrine, so I was fortunate to spend ample time away from the crowds of pilgrims. I also saw the Basilica several times during my stay, receiving much spiritual insight and a deep connection to my grandmother in Heaven, who had important messages for me.

So many other sacred sites around the world connect us intimately with the element of water.

When travelling to various sacred sites in and around Ireland, I accessed the healing power of water from different sacred wells, particularly pertaining to Goddess Brigid. The source of water connection to me is one of great power, and I encourage you to view the element of water as a means to feed your soul with the nourishment it needs. Similar to how we water the seeds within a garden to flourish, we also need to nourish the seeds planted within ourselves—so that they, too can bloom in divine timing.

I have also spent time at the sacred Chalice Well in Glastonbury, England, known as the *Red Spring*. The Chalice Well sits at the base of the Glastonbury Tor and is considered the Isle of Avalon from Arthurian legend. According to legend, the Chalice Well is believed to have risen from the ground where the Chalice (The Holy Grail) that Jesus drank from at *The Last Supper* was, and drops of his blood were caught at his Crucifixion. I did not drink the water from this well (although I did gather some to bring home to Australia). It is said to look and taste like iron nails used at the Crucifixion. Legend has it that the Holy Grail was placed into the well and that many healing properties come from this sacred water.

There is also a second well nearby at the foot of the Glastonbury Tor, known as the *White Spring* which is rich in calcium.

I recall sitting in meditation in this space, and today I hold a particularly fond memory of my daughter, immersing herself within the energy here at the Chalice Well. It is a place of deep healing and inner peace.

There are many ways that you may incorporate the element of water into your everyday living, such as:

- Blessing the water you drink (Japanese Scientist Dr Emoto states that positive thinking can help strengthen your immune system and assist you in moving forward). As you hold your glass of water between your hands, think loving, positive words and thoughts into the water for which your body will benefit upon every nourishing sip;

- Luxuriate yourself in a bath filled with aromatic oils (refer to chapter 4) or rose petals, soft candle lighting and possibly your favourite relaxing music;
- Cleanse and purify your body in an ocean, river or lake and use the body of water as a way in which you may release and let go. You can also do this as a daily shower ritual and imagine letting go of all that no longer serves you as the water flows off your body. While at the same time observing and acknowledging that you are purifying your body as well as your mind and spirit.

Water teaches us about the ebb and flow of life and how we may honour every cycle of nature within our lives. Any opportunity you have to be beside a body of water, allow this element's intuitive mystery to gift you nurturing of the Goddess within.

I invite you to get curious as to other ways you can be creative with the elements of nature (particularly that of water, but also that of air, fire and earth) to enhance your life as a woman moving forward.

- Where is it that you feel most relaxed in nature?
- Which locations do you feel your intuition as a woman is heightened?

Aromatherapy Connection

Many essential oils allow deep connection to the element of water and one of which is that of spearmint. This essential oil has a very herbaceous odour reminiscent of the crushed herb. This oil dates back to the Ancient Greeks, who often used it in their bath water.

Spearmint may bring a sense of calm within the chaos of life, allowing you to tune out to the noise of the world around you and tune inward to the silent whispers of the soul. This essential oil can bring about focus without too much overstimulation. It has less menthol concentration in it than peppermint and so has more of a gentle feeling to it energetically.

Remove the cap of your spearmint essential oil bottle and inhale its aroma. While doing so, visualise healing energies washing over your body and auric field and diving deep into the mysteries of life. Archangel Raphael (often referred to as the healing angel) may also be called upon when using this oil to help lift heavy emotions from your physical body to be transmuted.

While inhaling this refreshing scent, ask yourself the following questions:

- What lessons are you here to teach me?
- What gifts do you have to share with me?
- What do I need to acknowledge and accept within me so that I may move forward?

You may also use the above connection method in an oil diffuser or vaporiser.

Receive your guidance with an open heart and mind and return to this technique whenever you need to re-group, ground and re-focus your energies.

Spearmint is terrific, especially when you require a tender touch of love to uplift you; this is a beautiful way to use aromatherapy as a healing tool from the plant kingdom.

Crystal Connection

Aquamarine is a beautiful crystal connecting you to the element of water—the basis of all life. It helps to soothe and calm emotions and connect deeply to awaken the divine feminine.

This crystal has great depth; it's multilayered, much like we are as women. Aquamarine has dreamy energy, allowing you to sink into your intuitive feminine power. It will enable you to submerge the external world and all that is consciously known to you with the subconscious and internal world that perhaps you only choose to reveal to yourself or those close to you.

Aquamarine is also a powerful ally to assist you when the courage to overcome fears and anxiety is required.

Many other crystals may assist you in connecting deeply with the spirit of water. Another of my favourites is that of larimar, which is found in the Dominican Republic in the Caribbean Sea and strongly connects you with Atlantis and the hidden realms. Those with a solid connection to dolphins and whales are also attracted to this intuitive stone. I was fortunate to bring a piece of larimar home from my travels in the Caribbean many years ago. So my connection to the energies associated with this crystal is amplified.

Take the opportunity to meditate with the above crystals and allow your intuition to flow like waves upon the ocean. Hold your crystal in your hand, or lay down with the crystal gently resting upon your third eye and allow your intuitive messages to flow gently into your awareness.

Goddess Connection

Goddess Oshun is a Goddess of love, beauty and femininity. Women seeking assistance bearing children or dealing with infertility often call upon this wise river Goddess for fertile water assistance. Jewellery, perfume, dancing and seashells are sacred to this West African Goddess. She is also sought after in times of drought or severe poverty to have the rivers of life flourish abundantly.

When connecting with this Yoruba Goddess, who is thought to be as sweet as honey yet dangerous when crossed, be sure to love her deeply and be forever loyal, holding a deep respect for the wishes you seek and remembering your word is your wand.

Enhance the space within your home by devoting an altar to this Goddess with items like a jar of honey, sunflowers, oranges, cinnamon, pumpkin and peacock feathers to bring about prosperity, love and fertility.

Affirmation

"I am in tune with nature and the elements, as Mother Earth guides me to connect to my life purpose."

Seed #11

The connection to the elements of nature (especially water, given the womb is a woman's sacred chalice) and the natural world around you helps to align with the true essence of the glorious woman within.

Allow the earth to speak to you through the natural beauty of the world around you. Find ways to connect to Mother Earth daily and hear her words of wisdom.

Allow your creative, magical rhythm to flow through the sacred waters held within the container of your womb.

CHAPTER 12

The Sisterhood Movement

Our minds are constantly working overtime, particularly these days with so much on the go. What I find interesting regarding our stress levels is that we often live in the past or worry about the future, which only serves to heighten stress even further. Throughout this book, we have explored thought processes and their influence on us concerning the trauma stored within the body. The trauma held within our bodies stems from an emotional response that we then feel within our physical bodies. Emotions are energy-in-motion, meaning they need to move through us for us to move forward. Often we can be triggered in the current day by past emotions that we haven't been able to process, and the brain then sees the same pattern today in the same way it saw the original trauma.

When I was a young woman in my early twenties, I was not as self-assured as I am today. My confidence and self-esteem were often low, and when I finally met someone who loved me for me, I didn't think I was worthy of receiving this love or that the love would last. Looking back on it, I can see patterns of *abandonment* and the anxiety of not feeling good enough.

"If we could just move in together…he won't leave me". "If we could just get engaged…he won't leave me". "If we can just get married…he won't leave me". "If we could just have a baby…he won't leave me". It took me years to acknowledge the fear of abandonment that sat deep within me. This deep-rooted fear sat within me for lifetimes if I'm to be brutally honest with myself. We all have fears; it's a fact of life. Yet, if we let those fears take over, this is when the damage takes place and prevents us from living the best life we possibly can. The unnecessary fears I have mentioned above have nothing to do with my loving and ever-supportive husband or anyone else. The fears I held and the fears we all hold are the creation of the stories we tell ourselves, the often false narratives that play out in our minds of what could happen, but what, in truth, may also in fact, never happen. These fears that have played out in my mind throughout my life all stem from wanting to belong. To have someone close in my life who will never leave me, to be by my side forever and be loyal to me above all else.

I can see the patterns that have developed in my life where the fear of abandonment is a recurring theme. Loyalty to me is one of my top values in life. If you come into my life and spend time in my sacred space, I welcome you with open arms and an open and giving heart. In return, I desire the same level of trust, loyalty, respect and honour. There have been times in my life when I have held relationships with others, only to have betrayal, deceit, jealousy, backstabbing, secrecy, exclusion and pain, often resulting in a severing of these relationships or placing distance as a barrier to further hurt.

I am sure that I am not alone in many of the feelings I have expressed. Women are hard-wired for deep connection to other women. When that connection is severed due to bitter wounds, it cuts deeply and requires healing to move forward. As a woman, I have found that enduring this sense of pain, particularly at another woman's hand, is excruciating.

There is a place inside us that wants to feel a sense of belonging—belonging to a tribe of like-minded individuals and an inclusive group that offers a sense of belonging in the world as a whole. In my world, if you come into my life, I will stand by you, honour you, celebrate your wins, help you through any hardship, and love you for you. I am a person who will give my all to everything I do, and this also includes deep relationship connections. I see you for you, without judgment and without jealousy. In return, all I have ever wanted was to receive the same.

Through my work on the shadow self (the parts of our personality that we often would prefer not to have) and during my personal meditation practice, I feel that my fears of abandonment are the result of standing up for beliefs in times gone by that were not welcomed or supported by others and as a result, punishment of some description was endured as a way to disempower the woman within.

In the Dark Ages until the early 19th Century, so-called *witches* were burned at the stake. Often the healer, midwife or wise woman was seen as a threat to society and needed to be stopped at all costs. Women's power in healing often challenged the church institutions and were banned from educational opportunities. Women even betrayed one another to save themselves, which I believe is a catalyst for the reasoning behind why even today, among our society and all that we have learned from the past that unfortunately, some women still mistreat their fellow sisters to get ahead in their own life.

I witness that my personal fear of abandonment may be cultivated from being segregated, judged and at times thought less of as a result of pagan witchcraft influences of my past. I hold European ancestry, particularly French, English, Irish and Scottish. I observe that there may be past life patterns re-occurring today from these times. It is also quite possible that my deep connection to plant medicine for healing, following the cycles of nature and wholeheartedly believing in earth-based spirituality heralds from past life experiences too. We are all made up of so many vast experiences not only within this lifetime and the wisdom we find within our wounds but also that of past life experiences.

In my early years, I often felt that if I spoke my truth, it would come at a high cost, and it is something that I continue to work on even to this very day. Yet the difference nowadays is that I understand my worth as a woman and what I have to share with others that is important and valid, whether it is accepted or understood by others or not. These learned behaviour patterns are often ingrained from earlier trauma in our lives. You may relate to something of a similar nature. For instance, if when we were children, and we had to stand in front of the class to speak, and somebody mocked you or laughed or made you feel unworthy, it can then lead to a learned pattern of behaviour that triggers certain situations later in life of public speaking and that speaking your truth and that being heard comes with a cost of humiliation etc. Suppose you notice these patterns and triggers and witness that they are not serving you, the first step toward healing is to witness them and notice the emotion that comes up for you and where it sits within your body. Often when it comes to communication issues, it can sit in the throat, negatively impacting your throat chakra and the inability to speak your truth.

It is time to reclaim our power as women and cease competing with one another and instead unite as a whole. In turn, it enables women to heal the pain of DNA strands of shattered times when a woman would see a fellow sister as a threat to their livelihood and success.

I have felt alone on my spiritual journey for most of my life, a lone wolf if you like. Following a path of deep discovery of self is never easy, and when done solo, it's even more challenging. I am fortunate to have some very dear friends, many of whom have been in my life for decades. However, living a deeply spiritual life as I have chosen, can sometimes feel lonely, as the road to self is not always understood by others. In reading this book, I wish for you to know that even if you feel alone on your journey, there is always spirit by your side and many others in a similar position. Together, we are each cheering each other on.

When there is a passion inside of you to express everything you are feeling and want to share with the world, there is no stopping a woman. This power is strengthened through sisterhood, and I'm talking true sisterhood, where there is no competition; it is pure connection. A sisterhood of women who gather for a common goal of genuinely listening, supporting, sharing and growing as a group is one of the most powerful ways a woman can rise to her greatest capacity.

Being able to share deep experiences with other women is essential to me. Over the years, I have been fortunate to find specific individuals who truly understand and accept me for me. Some of these individuals do not even live in the same country as me. This is the beauty of technology and how easy it is to connect with like-minded souls across the globe in our modern world. Location is no longer a barrier to connectivity and soul connection.

There is a sense of achievement when women come together with a common thread to heal, grow and evolve. As one woman shares what's happening within her world and sits in a container of love, it enables her sisters to feel supported in doing the same. Sitting in a circle of non-judgment with heartfelt wishes for each sister around her helps a woman to continue her journey forward with golden threads of strength along her path. True sisterhood is not about trying to *fix* each other; it's about being heard and seen. Often, all women need from another is to say, "I see you and I hear you", and that's enough.

When we gather as a collective of women, we gather as one—as a united force for good, for love and abundance not only within our own lives but, in turn, abundance for the planet. Throughout a gathering of women, you may find that even though we all may come from different walks of life and have had different experiences throughout our time on this earth, the one common denominator is the deep-rooted desire to be of service to one another and help heal the wounds of humanity. When women share from an open heart sitting in the space of love, compassion, empathy and encouragement, we help lift one another up. Sharing our experiences, albeit different, we share the commonality of women helping to raise other women. There can be no greater desire than for another fellow human being to excel in all they do.

One of the most significant aspects I learned from my near-death experience is the value of love; ultimately, there truly is nothing more powerful than love, it sounds a little cliché, but from my personal experience through the veil, I can honestly say love conquers all.

Women are often made to play down their gifts, talents and abilities and have done so for centuries. Women have been made to feel they are in competition when it can't be further from the truth. When we sit together with one another, heart to heart, from a place of equality and love, we truly learn what the gift of sisterhood is.

Finding the right group of individuals can sometimes feel like a challenge. Sometimes we may feel like we are finally heard, only to find that others want to hear more of their voice than their sisters. When we find common ground among a group of women who understand us and allow us to be ourselves, whole and complete, without judgment or jealousy, we can rise beyond measure.

Please break down the barriers that may be held inside from times when you may not have felt heard or included or what you said mattered. I invite you to find a circle of women who support you through happy and challenging times and congratulate you on your successes. A sisterhood is full of genuine support toward you that also aids you through your sorrows. We rise and fall no matter our backgrounds, but when we can open our hearts to be alongside other sisters for the greater good of the whole, we know we have found true sisterhood.

One of the aspects I love about facilitating women's circles is the broad scope of lateral learning that takes place when women gather for a common goal of connection. The conversations in these kinds of gatherings differ from that of general coffee shop conversations with a friend about general life. These gatherings are always deep and meaningful, leaving you with a sense of fulfilment and rich discovery of who you are at your core and what you wish to bring into your world. I love the tapestry that seems to unfold with synchronicity too. Women can gather from all different walks of life, yet common threads pool us together at a similar time. You can always guarantee that someone within the circle will likely say something that resonates deep within you. This is the beauty of having a circle of sisters to sit with, share, and listen to. In a world that so often can be fuelled by competition and a constant rise to the top mentality, knocking each other down along the way, it is a welcome breath of fresh air. Gathering true sisters together brings no competition; it is pure heart-to-heart, soul-to-soul connection with the purest intentions to wish each other well.

When you find your tribe of women, hold them close and cherish the moments you share, as they are pure gold.

As a coach, an aspect of women that brings me such joy is seeing a woman shine her light and realise that she too, is worthy of being heard and seen for all she is. This doesn't often come easily, and the path of healing can sometimes be arduous. Having the willingness is the first step toward seeking ownership of your life and living out as the woman you were born to be which will gift the greatest of rewards.

As a women's circle facilitator, one of the areas that I love bringing into circles is the aspect of ritual and ceremony. This enables women to escape from ordinary time and into a time rich with ancient remembering and divine feminine leadership.

I recall a powerful gathering of women where my client, Penny, felt a little disconnected from life and daily happenings with friends and family. She was feeling at a low ebb and couldn't shake the lethargy for life. Penny was usually such an upbeat lady; to see her feeling so depressed with little zest for life was saddening. On this particular evening, as a group we undertook a powerful ritual connecting to our womb space and feeling the connection of our ancestor's support around us in meditation. Penny contacted me the next day expressing her deep gratitude and a slight bewilderment saying that while she couldn't explain it, "something had dramatically changed inside of me during the ritual" she said that she now felt back in her body and back in the world. This particular meditation also had aspects of travelling to Machu Picchu and the power of this sacred site in connection to the sacral chakra in particular. If you recall, in chapter 7, we explored the relationship with the chakras of the body in relation to the chakras of the world. I encourage you to explore chapter 7 and the associated mudras in detail, as their effects are profound, as Penny can attest.

Are you ready to find yourself within a circle of sisters who have your back no matter what is happening in your life? A circle of women who truly listen, without judgment and interruption? How often do you find in general conversations that you may begin to speak and only get cut off by another person wanting to be heard over you, as their life seems more important? A sisterhood community spirit is that where each woman is equal, there is no higher status. One woman might be facilitating; however, each woman is given an equal opportunity to be heard and seen—something that is not always felt in the outside world.

As a coach, I have found many women say that it is not always easy to find girlfriends who are on the same page when on a deep spiritual path. We are all awakening at various levels through life; those women who have chosen to accelerate faster often feel alienated and isolated. We need not go through our spiritual ascension and acceleration alone; however, we need to know when we are ready to find that gathering of like-minded women and how to seek one that resonates with you.

Every circle may be different. Some women's circles gather upon the moon's cycles and celebrate the current phase and the guidance of what each phase brings. Other circles may focus on areas of spiritual teachings, share healings such as Reiki or gather at changing sabbats through the wheel of life. There is no set rule of how a circle may run, and some women like to share the load and rotate as a circle facilitator, which can be lots of fun too. Today, we are also fortunate to have online sisterhood gatherings, which can be immensely rewarding, all in the comfort of your own home. I regularly participate in online communities of women, and the connection feels equal, as if they were sitting in the same room side by side.

The intention behind what you do is paramount. So I welcome you to search within and see if you feel ready to honour the part in you that seeks to be a part of a community of women helping to raise the vibration personally and for one another and, ultimately, the planet.

Another aspect of a sisterhood gathering that I love facilitating is incorporating spiritual craft. When groups of women gather and undertake a craft project (be it large or small), the conversations bring on a life of their own. The ease of letting your guard down and feeling safe to share from the heart opens. It is what women in ancient times would do while the men would go *hunt and gather*; the women would remain behind and look after the children and undertake such tasks as weaving baskets or creating spiritual adornments for ceremonies or rites of passage. These are often long-forgotten yet much needed aspects of a woman's life, and bringing these back into our lives through rituals and gatherings of a sisterhood helps us remember those old times. These times are ingrained in our souls; we remember them when we re-enact and connect on a soul level to other women within our tribe of modern-day gatherings.

Consider the following questions relating to your own life as a modern-day woman with the following questions:

- Do you hear the call to reclaim the essence of who you are as a woman in the modern world?
- Are you ready to empower yourself and help empower others in a safe and nurturing environment?
- Are you ready to gain clarity and confidence in your life?
- Are you willing to release your inner fears and take a step closer to love?
- Are you ready to deepen your intuition?
- Are you ready to cultivate deep soul-centred friendships?

If you answered yes to any of the above questions, I would welcome you to start your journey toward seeking a circle in person or in the online space to assist you. There has never been a more critical time on the planet for women to share their wisdom and to feel the nurturing, safe support of other women helping to raise the consciousness around us.

It's time to get out your journal (something I highly recommend my clients use when they attend sisterhood gatherings) and get to know yourself more intimately.

Suppose you were to find a group or tribe of women to call your own as a part of your sisterhood gathering. In that case, it's a great idea to review your current situation and your life as a whole. Asking questions is an excellent way to get to know yourself better. Choose to use this exercise below as an opportunity to put pen to paper (yes, the old-fashioned way, as it gets the creative juices flowing by activating both sides of the brain hemispheres). Above all else, be truthful; no one else needs to read your responses but you, so go for it!

Questions to ponder:

- If I were to meet you for the first time, what would you have me know about you?
- What do you see as your finest strengths in life?
- What are your deepest fears?
- How would a friend or family member describe you?
- How would you describe yourself?
- What are your gifts, talents and abilities and are you using them to your full advantage?
- When you were a child, what did you love to spend time doing?
- What can you do for yourself to bring even more light and love into your life?
- What are your goals, and where do you see yourself in 1, 5, or 10 years?
- If you were to look back upon your life at the end of your days here on earth, is there anything you regret not doing? If so, is there anything you may change now to create an opportunity to fulfil these now?

Sometimes it helps to journal or ask yourself deep questions such as the ones above and use this as an opportunity to analyse exactly what you are seeking, particularly in finding a circle of women to call your own.

I knew that attending Denise Linn's *Red Lotus Mystery School* was to form a part of my future, and I knew that a part of my future was helping women to see, feel and realise their worth. During my time in California, I reconnected more intimately to the divine feminine aspect within me, allowing me to discover ways to reclaim my inner Goddess. We all seek fulfilment in various ways, and for me, spiritual fulfilment has always been one of my top values. In my role as a coach, healer and spiritual teacher (be it in person or the online space), my light comes alive with women's group work, for when we help to heal one, we heal many. The power that emanates from a circle of women gathering with a common goal is immeasurable.

There have been countless times when women have gathered in circle with me and have felt such warmth and inner stirrings of the soul that they do not want to leave the space! Close bonds and friendships have been formed by group members outside of these circles, some of which may continue to be lifelong. This feeling of being filled from the inside and having our cup of self-care filled to the brim does wonders for the soul. Each circle builds upon the other and you begin to feel the sense of belonging that is so needed in today's society. These gatherings of united women allow us to go back into our lives using the inner strength that has been ignited and in turn magnetise a life you love.

Often all we need as women is a loving sister who sees us for who we are and loves us unconditionally. Sometimes we need to find ourselves on our own before we are ready to allow others to share the experiences of our journey with us. There can be great lessons from a solitary pursuit of spiritual discovery until we are ready to connect with other women on a similar path. As a woman, knowing what feels right for you is your sense of personal empowerment. There can be much to learn from a solo spiritual journey. Still, I know first-hand that it can also be challenging with nobody to understand what you may be going through as you travel the road through your rites of passage. Understanding that you are not alone and that many may be experiencing many shifts within of a similar solo nature can be reassuring. The solo journey of self has its own unique qualities and for the most part, many of us as women may shy away from the space of women's circles due to past conditionings and patterns of behaviour with lifetime after lifetime of having our sense of worth stifled or punished for speaking our truth. It is only now that sisterhood is rising stronger. Women are starting to understand the strength that may be brought to ourselves and the empowerment of those around us when we bond as a united front for the good of all.

There are many benefits of a sisterhood movement, such as:
- Ability to be seen and heard
- Accessing collective wisdom
- Bringing a sense of alignment to the rhythms and cycles of life as a woman
- Creating a safe space in which to learn, grow and evolve
- Deepening connection to self and others
- Support of like-minded souls

As women, we are hard-wired for connection to ourselves and other women; we seek that sense of belonging to a tribe and having a safe space much like that of the Moon Lodges and Red Tents of old to embrace life as a woman fully.

Within is a deep desire for connection, to belonging and seeking a sisterhood of companions. Harbouring emotional, mental or spiritual pain can inhibit your ability to fully embrace your inner Goddess and the life you wish to lead. You may consider where this pain has built up within your womb space and seek to release it.

Consider creating time and space to journal and delve a little deeper into patterns of conditioning within your life, the possible energy strands of your ancestors, and the consciousness of women across the globe, and how this may be blocking you from living fully and embracing your womanly essence.

- Where is it in your life that you may have felt a sense of abandonment?
- Have there been situations where you have not felt heard by others?
- Do you feel like there have been times when you have not been seen for the woman you are?
- What inner negative holding patterns and inner wounds are you ready to release from within your womb?

Aromatherapy Connection

As a facilitator, one of the ways that I love women in a group to commence connection to one another is through anointing.

You may choose to use the following ritual for a personalised one just for yourself, or it may be used in a group gathering situation.

The act of anointing is to apply essential oils to the skin where they may be easily absorbed and can be a beautiful self-love ritual.

I have created an anointing oil blend called "Trinity of Love" which consists of the following essential oils:

Jasmine is an oil that helps you feel comfortable with both your masculine and feminine sides (and we need both for balance and harmony within). It also helps us connect to our sacral chakra to birth new beginnings. This oil is a beautiful unification of both aspects of the masculine and feminine.

Frankincense is known as the king of oils. This oil connects us to our crown chakra and assists us to come back in alignment with the truth of who we are at our core essence. It can help eradicate the negative aspects of patriarchal energy by using it to heal relationships within the divine masculine and amplify the energy of enlightenment.

Rose is an oil that has long been associated with love and beauty. It is an essence that connects you with your heart chakra opening to your heart's desires. You may harness the qualities within to access your ability to love who you are and bloom in your own way and time.

Decades ago, I recall my aromatherapy lecturer drilling into us as students the phenomenal amount of steam distilling required from the petals of thousands of roses, even to get 5ml of rose essential oil. It's no wonder that rose essential oil is so expensive, yet so profoundly exquisite and worth every cent!

No other flower has been used for so many sacred purposes throughout history than the rose. Its blossom symbolises many aspects, including beauty, love and immortality. As a woman, I love the analogy of life starting as a tiny bud and then blossoming throughout every rite of passage until we reach our crone years and watch as this beautiful flower transforms during every stage of life.

Rose comforts us in times of need and soothes feelings of fear and anxiety by wrapping you in a blanket of love through its scent.

Combining the trinity of the above oils creates a beautiful option to use as an anointing oil.

Pre-prepare the above blend mixed with a carrier oil of your choice and place it within a roller bottle for ease of use time and time again. This roller bottle will also hold the energies of its use throughout sisterhood gatherings or your own desire to find a sisterhood in the time to come.

In a 10ml roller bottle, place your choice of carrier oil (e.g. almond oil, apricot oil, jojoba oil) mixed with the following essential oils:

> "Trinity of Love"
> - 2 drops of jasmine
> - 2 drops of frankincense
> - 2 drops of rose
> - 2 teaspoons of carrier oil

Ritual:

Take three deep and full breaths into the body; if in group, turn and face your fellow sister and ask if she would like to receive the gift of anointing. If so, place a hand on your heart and gaze soulfully into her eyes and say the following words:

"(*Insert the name of sister*) from my heart and womb to yours, welcome sister", and roll the oil onto your finger and gently anoint your sister's third eye (please note this area of the body can be particularly sensitive so always use light pressure over the third eye). Then embrace your fellow sister with a warm hug as she then passes the roller blend to the sister beside her. Continue this until all sisters have been welcomed into circle.

If anointing for personal use, you may still follow a similar pattern through the breath, only this time connecting to your heart, womb and soul. You may anoint your heart space, the hollow of your throat and even your wrists to bathe in the aromatic scent of the Trinity of Love energies.

Crystal Connection

The beautiful green and pink stone from South Africa, unakite may assist you with friendships and creating more self-love. Therefore, it is a lovely choice to help open the awareness to finding a tribe of fellow sisters that will aid your mission of speaking from the heart among nurturing, supportive souls.

It is also a stone of vision, helping to balance emotions and spirituality.

You may place a small tumbled piece of unakite upon your third eye when laying down in meditation to help bring insights regarding past blockages that may be inhibiting your spiritual growth. Unakite can be used as an aid in getting to the source of the issue and helping to bring it to the surface so that it may allow for transformation and transmutation.

Goddess Connection

Artemis is a wonderful Goddess to connect to regarding friendships and finding a sisterhood community. Artemis is the Goddess of the hunt and the moon and is a protector of women, adolescent girls and animals—also an excellent Goddess to call upon with fertility and childbirth.

Spending time in nature is a perfect way in which to connect with Goddess Artemis, especially through the woodlands. If you can remove your shoes and feel the earth beneath your feet, you will feel all the better for it! I regularly love to go barefoot on the earth and feel the vibrational healing of Mother Earth supporting me.

Artemis is often depicted with a bow and arrow. So symbolically, you may picture yourself with your own bow and arrow on the hunt to find your tribe of fellow sisters to unite with.

Affirmation

"I open my heart and womb, allowing a fellowship of nurturing sisterhood to fill the cup of my soul."

Seed #12

There is a sense of deep belonging within our society through connection to a group of like-minded women. A sense of belonging enables us to feel a part of the global consciousness toward a knowingness and understanding that women may help other women rise and in turn, bring about our sense of empowerment. Encouragement, support and inspiration is a key aspect of the sisterhood movement, which is growing and rising stronger than ever before.

CHAPTER 13

Living the Way of the Goddess

Often a familiar feeling among women when they gather for ritual and ceremony, particularly in groups, is the feeling that they have been there before; it all feels very familiar, like they have undertaken rituals and ceremonies of a similar nature in the past. One of my clients, in particular, would often feel a sense of remembering when she would come to see me for one-on-one healings of a shamanic nature. Cate would often state to me, "I feel like we've been here before". We would regularly experience aspects of ancient remembering between us of times gone by when for instance, I was a high priestess bestowing the ancient rites to those women around me. A high priestess is deeply connected to the divine, often born into royalty and oversees sacred rituals and ceremonies. She is also one who can teach others through her own experiences and personal journey, enabling her to impart knowledge to her fellow initiates. Perhaps you may have feelings or emotions stirred within you of times when you may have taken on the archetype of the high priestess? We will explore more about archetypes within this chapter.

The more I step further into my aspect of living the way of the Goddess, the more the ancient remembering stirs within me. I can bring this ancient wisdom into modern-day times to assist women in reclaiming their femininity as a whole. You may start to do this also as you connect more deeply from hereon to ancient ways and rituals now that you have brought it into your conscious awareness.

By invoking the ways of the Goddess within you, it helps to align you with the truth of who you are, not only as a woman but as an integral part of the evolution of Mother Earth.

If every woman were made aware of the mysteries of womanhood from an early age as a rite of passage into womanhood, we would be far more apt to deal with life as a whole with greater ease.

So many women I have coached over the years or who have come to me for healing, particularly womb healing, struggle with the complexities behind the concept of what being a woman means and the potential held within the container of their womb as a means in which to create. As more and more people in our society start to awaken and become aware of their inner potential, the more they may begin to magnetise a life they love.

Through the various circles and workshops I have offered over the years, I have noticed the power and intensity grow within the community and global consciousness toward wholehearted living and the rise in the awareness of the Goddess herself.

More women are starting to place a higher value on their need for self-care as an essential part of everyday living instead of viewing it as a luxury or selfish *treat*. It also means the more they are accelerating at a faster speed toward spiritual evolvement and ways to help serve humanity as a whole.

Most women are a combination of many divine feminine archetypes. It has been my endeavour that the three main female archetypes of maiden (with attributes of carefree innocence and spirited youth), mother (the nurturer of self and others), and crone (the wise woman who accepts and owns all of who she is) have been brought closer to your attention throughout this book and a deeper understanding of how they impact your life in powerful and positive ways. These feminine archetypes do not end here, as the concept of archetypes opens a new level of awareness of the different qualities and personality traits within our human psyche.

There are other archetypes that I wish to bring your focus and awareness on your travels through the journey of womanhood and the divine feminine. You may resonate with some or many of these, and I have found that working with these archetypes (and others that are not mentioned within this chapter but you may wish to explore further) brings a new level of understanding to relationships. Relationships that relate both with yourself as the courageous woman that you are and also the relationships that you have with those around you and how you may bring compassion and understanding towards all that comes your way.

Priestess:

The archetype of the priestess is one where a woman feels wholly absorbed in the understanding that life can be sacred and can have profound spiritual lessons along the journey. Still, she also understands that life can sometimes be *ordinary* and finds a way to merge the two together in unison.

It becomes an attribute and exquisite quality in which this unison gives form to her becoming a natural-born leader of spiritual wisdom and insight, whether in a traditional teaching format or an informal discussion among friends. By drawing upon the aspects of the priestess, life is fulfilled through divine connection and in doing so, people naturally gravitate toward her.

In times gone by through history, the women with this archetype in their psyche have often been persecuted for being who they are, which is why many women today who feel the deep desire for the priestess within them to come out may shy away in fear of another wave of this cause of action.

A priestess has a deep calling to serve and impart her wisdom of all she has ever learned to those around her.

Within your own life, I'd like you to take a moment to consider how the archetype of priestess may come into play. Are you the one your girlfriends turn to for advice, be it health-related, relationships or general help? Or maybe you notice who the woman is in your social circles that is sought out as the *go-to* for answers about life's questions. It's interesting to note how the various feminine archetypes play out. It's important to remember that we can turn all aspects of multiple archetypes on within our lives as women depending upon when we need them.

Ultimately the priestess dives deep into the unseen world through connection to the divine; she knows and understands herself and lives and breathes through her intuition by embodying the sacredness of being a woman.

Goddess example: Pythia

Queen:

The archetype of the queen is one of wise leadership, sovereignty and a strong loyalty to those around her. She often indulges in the finer luxuries that life offers, and there is certainly no wrong with this. A part of owning the queen archetype within is to understand that when life gifts you opportunities to lavish in luxury, particularly an abundance of wealth, it is also an opportunity to witness where you may be of service more in your life in fair exchange for this abundance.

Too often, women in society may feel threatened by a woman in such a position that the queen holds. However, the queen usually has significant burdens that are only sometimes public knowledge. We do not always know what a woman may go through in her life, so honouring and respecting where each of us may be on our journey is crucial to our evolution and ability to enhance how we live as an embodiment of our inner Goddess.

The queen is a woman in her power as opposed to power over others. She understands that she is being guided by a source far more significant than herself and can tune into this power to bring strength to those around her as she lives out her purpose.

Goddess example: Hera

The Warrior:

The energy of this particular archetype is a woman who knows what she wants, is independent and goes after her quest with the essence of the warrior spirit within. She is confident, ambitious and a driving force of nature in pursuing her goals and achieving them passionately and purposefully.

Think of wonder woman, fighting battles and taking on the world. She's independent, strong and goal-oriented and trusts herself completely.

Goddess examples: Artemis, Diana, Ishtar

The Sage:

She is the wise woman within, seeking knowledge and understanding and using this wisdom to teach, mentor and guide others along their path. The sage is a seeker of truth and often leads into introspection to review, analyse and deeply accept where she is on her path along with all that she has learnt and discovered.

Goddess examples: Athena, Durga, Freyja, Inanna, Ishtar, Lileth

The Mystic:

This archetype focuses on inner fulfilment with a sense of mystery and dreaminess about her. She is a seeker of freedom, inner peace and mystery. She is one to seek out the sacred in all that she does.

Goddess examples: Hestia, Vesta

The Lover:

The lover archetype seeks passionate connection, whether in the sense of a life partner or a devoted love for a cause she wholeheartedly believes in. It's a sense of giving and receiving deep love. Looking at the wounds we are holding provides us with an opportunity to witness the little girl inside of us and get in touch with her needs and sense of belonging. Often what triggers us today is a deep-rooted need to heal a part of ourselves as a child. The lover archetype fully knows her body and how to express her sensuality and sexuality.

Goddess examples: Aphrodite, Venus, Oshun, Inanna, Hathor

We must always remember that, as with nature, there is always light and dark; therefore, all archetypes also have their shadow side. Some examples of the shadow side of the above archetypes are:

Maiden: obedient, attached, people pleasing

Mother: over-giving, controlling, co-dependent

Crone: can struggle with vulnerability, emotions and sexual expression

Priestess: can struggle to trust own intuition, perfectionism

Queen: judgemental, image-conscious, jealous

Warrior: uncontrollable anger, vengeful, win-at-all-costs mentality

Lover: irresponsible, non-committal, obsessive

With the introduction to archetypes, you may notice the energies that resonate within you and also the ones that trigger you. Witness these, and I encourage you to explore these further and begin to start leading from your body, your feminine wisdom and your inner truth. We can begin reflecting on the qualities we already use and the ones we may wish to cultivate more of. You may wish to deepen your connection to the Goddess examples within the archetypes that I have presented you with.

Taking care of the home you reside in is a fabulous way to connect particularly to the mother archetype within your psyche. Our homes create a safe sanctuary for us to retreat, heal and transform. Our homes are our sanctuary, providing us with safety to be ourselves. Our homes, indeed, are a reflection of us, and harnessing the qualities of the feminine archetypes together with aligned action allows your home's energy to nurture every aspect of womanhood.

One of the fastest ways to embrace and live the way of the Goddess is through clearing your clutter. While writing this book, my home(s) underwent influential periods of clutter clearing (where every room in the house changed in some format, including the purpose and focus of certain rooms). The art of clutter clearing helped pave the way toward the completion of my manuscript and to define who I am as a Goddess within the modern world we live in. I regularly undertake the powerful exercise of clutter clearing. Each time it still amazes and astounds me what is cleared from my home, which in turn creates a gateway of opportunity for new energy to come my way and give rise to a new level of myself as a woman.

When we shift the energy within our space, we equally change the energy within ourselves, these aspects are so divinely entwined.

Are you ready to step closer to living the way of the Goddess every day? Start to investigate your home and how it relates to you now and how you may seek to instigate change so that it reflects the woman you truly are.

While there may be physical clutter within your home, it is not always the tangible objects; in fact, if we were to delve deeper, it's perhaps never really about the physical objects, more the deeper meaning we place upon them.

Having worked with multitudes of clients over the years, I know the act of clutter clearing is an integral component in helping shape your way forward in the world. I know first-hand how powerful it can be. From a personal perspective, I recall several years ago, a room in my home that I didn't particularly appreciate when it came to clutter clearing. The room itself (a spare room) looked neat and tidy, but if I were to delve deeper into the cupboards, it held a lot of memorabilia about the past (old photo albums, old toys, paperwork, old electrical items and more), plus it had also been the room in which I had miscarried our first child. Therefore, this particular room held a residual energy of grief, energies of the past and emotional holding. Of all the rooms within our home, this is the one place that, although on a surface level, looked clutter-free, the deeper I delved, the more emotion there was. I have found that clutter clearing can sometimes feel a little confronting, intense and emotional. Still, on the flip side of the coin, there is a sense of joy, relief and release that comes from being free of constraints that are often placed unknowingly upon ourselves. As I regularly take on the task of clutter-clearing my home (as I know and feel the benefits on many levels), I am proud to say that the energy within this room has shifted. The emotional charge it once had upon me has moved to a higher vibrational level.

Take an opportunity to venture around your home and investigate what is sitting within the cupboards and underneath the beds. Often times clutter can be hidden away from view and yet still impacts you and your energy field. Much like pushing down, suppressing and repressing our inner wounds impacts our life, so too does our clutter.

My daughter moved bedrooms in the family home during the early stages of writing this book. There were many objects that she clutter cleared in preparation for her new room, together with holding onto items she was not ready to part with (but not wanting them to be physically in her new space). Holding onto the past is fine if it is done with loving intent. Boxing up old toys and placing a rose quartz or selenite crystal inside the box can keep the energy vibration high and help release the energy strands of the past until you are ready to part with the items altogether if need be.

There certainly isn't anything wrong with holding onto objects that are special to you and that you love, but if you do not love it or use it, you may consider getting rid of it or donating it. I have found over the years that objects I may not have released in the past in the next round of clutter clearing, I have been able to part with more ease as the charge or hold over me was no longer as strong. When you are going through objects that you are not ready to part with, it may be that you set an intention that if this box hasn't been opened in six months, twelve months (or whatever length of time you choose), then it may be time for you to consider the option of moving it on either recycling where possible, selling it or giving it away.

As women, many of us can hoard clothing or shoes we do not use. With clothing, it can be that you paid a lot of money for it; it may remind you of a time in the past, an aspiration to be a dress size less or something else. A great way in which to clear the wardrobe for clothes you are yet to part with is to put it on the clothes hanger the opposite way around; when you next take up the opportunity to clear your clutter and find that it is still hanging the wrong way, it sends a more vital message to you that perhaps you really don't need this item and are now ready to make way for new energy to stream through.

If you are going to look toward clutter clearing, two of the most intimate places for you to seek positive change is your bedroom and your bathroom. Your bedroom is a place that you spend an enormous amount of time in, it's where you recharge your batteries at the end of a long day, and it's where you dream your life into being. Therefore, this is the place that will have a significant impact on your life, so I suggest taking the opportunity to look here first. You then follow closely with the bathroom. A bathroom is a place of purification and honouring your body with the daily bathing ritual; therefore, you will want this space to be as free of clutter as possible so that you are not holding any stagnant, emotional water energy.

A client of mine, Amanda, had just been through the trauma of a nasty divorce, and she was continuously waking up each morning feeling depleted despite what should have been a decent length of sleep. I asked her to tell me about her bedroom and the objects she had in there. A little bewildered at first, she went on to speak to me about her room, and we discovered that on her dresser she had a small jewellery box given to her by her ex-husband as an anniversary gift one year, and inside the box was an inscription "Happy Anniversary–I love you today, tomorrow and always". This jewellery box, while seemingly insignificant, was an object in Amanda's line of vision every night before sleep and every morning upon waking. I asked her how she felt about it. She said that the box always made her blood boil and that whenever she opened the box for her jewellery, she snickered in disgust and anger at his meaningless, empty words and how he'd since moved on with another woman. She also had a lot of other items in her bedroom needing some clutter-clearing attention and storage of unloved goods under the bed. By shifting the energy within her bedroom and releasing things that did not make her feel good, she started sleeping restfully at night, waking with a refreshed and renewed attitude toward life and the woman she desired to be. She no longer held onto this unresolved pain within the storehouse of her womb and body.

What or where in your life do you need to clear the space within your home? I invite you to give yourself some time to walk around your home with intention. Just noticing what makes you feel invigorated, brings a smile to your face and lights you up while also seeing what or where in your home diminishes your energy. Living the way of the Goddess extends to your home space also as it is an extension of your energy and the way you portray yourself to the world.

I have found that clutter clearing is a continual process of change. As we grow on our path, we gather new items and ways of being within our home, and therefore we outgrow other aspects. You may include clutter clearing as a seasonal cycle reflection, recharging and re-energising your space as the year unfolds. We live in a world of constant change, so our personal space needs to also reflect this. Embrace change, embrace your life and allow your inner Goddess to shine.

There is an Archangel whom I love to call upon when I am in clutter-clearing mode—Archangel Jophiel. She acts as your own personal Feng Shui consultant. You may also add extra support from the spirit realm by calling upon her for extra assistance with your clutter clearing.

One aspect I must highlight within you regarding clearing your clutter is to do so with intention. The intention behind your clearing is the extra sense of power behind the magic. You may also do this with mundane tasks like cleaning the house by using affirmations such as "*As I clear and cleanse my home, I bring further clarity into my life*" and bringing in the intent that as you clean your home, you also clean and clear your energy, making way for fresh, vibrant and uplifting energy to come your way. You may choose to create your own affirmation depending on what you wish to enhance or release from your life.

Living the way of the Goddess starts and finishes with you. You choose how you view your world and the people and items that frequent your energy field. Living the way of the Goddess is also about remembering that you are not trying to be anyone else but yourself, whole and complete. Allowing yourself to remove the masks you place upon yourself and having a home that truly reflects you deepens your trust that who you are as a woman is enough.

Stepping out in the world around you as your inner Goddess allows you to own your truth and who you are at your core. Living the way of the Goddess means showing up every day in your power, from your thoughts upon waking to the way you bring sacredness to a simple everyday routine such as bathing, the way you choose to dress, the way you hold your physical body when you move, the language you use when you communicate to another. Living the way of the Goddess doesn't mean that you won't make mistakes or get angry or sad sometimes or that there won't be challenges or trauma along the way—but it is about embracing all that life has to offer, both the highs and the lows.

When you show up each day with the intent to be the best version of yourself possible, this is what living the way of the Goddess entails. It's about remembering that no matter how many times you may fall, it's the ability to keep going and rising above that counts. Living the way of the Goddess can, at times, allow you to be a fierce and strong warrior with the courage to conquer all battles. However, it can also be your sense of grace, beauty, deep wisdom and love of all surrounding you. Inside, you hold the qualities of the great Goddess, the one who encompasses the whole of humanity with an array of attributes and archetypes to display to the world in your own unique and perfect way.

You were born into this world with a unique purpose and mission, and it is your calling alone. Stop trying to be somebody else and continue the path chosen for you to walk.

Living the way of the Goddess is also the understanding that we are never seeking answers outside of ourselves. There are many aspects of the Goddess, do not be afraid of using every part of you to express who you are; you truly can make a difference, not only in your life but in the lives of many, simply by being yourself. When you are in alignment with what captures the essence of your heart and soul, this is what gives rise to stepping through the gateway of Goddess wisdom.

One of the most significant aspects of living the Goddess's way is the self-care you bring to yourself as a woman and honouring the creative chalice of your womb. When you enter the Goddess gateway as a means of wholehearted living, it also entails embracing your womb as the sacred vessel of birthing all that you desire as a woman in the modern world.

Aromatherapy Connection

I grew to love and adore the oil bergamot while first studying for my aromatherapy diploma in my early days as a therapist. Its combination of bitter orange and lemon scent called me home to my inner sorcerer or alchemist (the art of divine magic). It is also the special ingredient note of Earl Grey tea. Drawing upon my English ancestry, I have always had a fondness for Earl Grey. When connecting Earl Grey with bergamot, my appreciation grew even further. I have spent many a lifetime working with lotions and potions and plant medicine for healing. It is my wish for you that the aromatherapy information shared within this book has sparked your interest for using the plant kingdom for healing also.

Bergamot allows you to bring in a sense of calm and contentment while also assisting in removing fears. It is a beautiful oil that women may utilise to help reclaim their inner power.

I suggest you give your feet a gentle, nurturing massage before retiring to bed. Bergamot can be helpful as a way to prepare your body for sleep as it has sedative qualities, unlike most citrus essential oils, which tend to be more uplifting and energising. Since the pores on the feet are some of the largest on the body, it enables the essential oils to penetrate efficiently and effectively through the skin and benefit the whole body.

Blend bergamot with your choice of carrier oil (such as almond or apricot oil) to create a nurturing blend for your feet. Like most other essential oils, please note that bergamot should always be diluted in a carrier oil instead of applied neatly to the skin.

I have put together the following blend for you as a ritual before preparing for sleep and further invoking your inner Goddess in your dream state.

- 2 drops of bergamot
- 2 teaspoons of carrier oil (e.g. almond oil)

Your entire body, mind and soul will reap the benefits from nurturing your feet through massage. You can also use the power of intention to program a night of restful sleep ahead, focusing on reclaiming your power as a woman.

Crystal Connection

The crystal and mineral kingdom allows us to work with earth energy and bring healing properties into our everyday life.

The final crystal I want you to explore and bring into your awareness is actually a fossil—ammonite. An ammonite has the power to connect you deep into the earth. I first fell in love with ammonite while travelling to Glastonbury, experiencing the power of the divine feminine energy at the Chalice Well and its surrounds. An ammonites' unique spiral formation reflects the specific frequencies the divine feminine holds. Ammonite energy has deep ancient wisdom, much like the wisdom we each carry inside of us, awaiting the spiral dance to unleash the Goddess within.

An ammonite is a group of shelled cephalopods that became extinct about 66 million years ago. They bring a powerful and potent union between the mineral and animal kingdoms. Due to the fact they come from the ocean, they emit qualities of the feminine such as intuition, our emotional body and the unconscious.

Due to their deep connection to the past, they can be incredibly connected to past lives, our ancestors, spirit guides and the wisdom received through the ages. However, they also allow you to gain a higher perspective by reviewing the past, considering the future, and being fully present with the here and now.

The spiral represents the ever-turning cycle of life with birth, death and rebirth and our connection to the rhythm and cycles in our lives. They also historically were used for fertility, pregnancy and childbirth. Given that they come from the ocean, the connection to the moon and to the womb is strong.

Connect with an ammonite in meditation by resting a small piece upon your third eye. The purchase of an ammonite pendant on a necklace is quite popular, so wearing one may also enhance your appreciation for life as it transmutes negative energy and helps open yourself to your inner wisdom.

Goddess Connection

The Greek Goddess Gaia will complete our journey together as an introduction to further connect with the Goddess within. She is closely related to earth energy and allows you to slow down, witness all that is occurring in your life and remain present in your body. There can be a tendency for many of us on the spiritual journey to want to accelerate at rapid speeds, at times this may create unease within the physical body. Connecting with Gaia helps you bring conscious awareness to self and how you may nurture your body, mind and spirit with the aid of nature.

Enable yourself to be grounded daily with the loving and supportive assistance of the earth's mother, Gaia.

The ability to simply *be* and immerse yourself in nature regularly will help connect you to our earth mother.

I recall a time that my family and I travelled to Romania. It was a bitterly cold winter, and the snow was heavy. I would often be called to a location throughout our travels, not knowing why and yet listening to my intuition. This one particular travel experience took us well off the beaten path, so much so that our experienced tour guide was not even sure that our vehicle would make it as the roads may not be open due to the depth of snow. Let alone the place I had wanted us to explore he had never even heard of and on the map it appeared to be beyond the end of the road. We set off in search of Monastery Rupestra in Sinca Veche, which I was called by the divine to attend. Travelling the long and lonely roads throughout the Romanian countryside, often stopping to ask local gypsies directions, we finally made it. The car stopped, and we got out in the crisp, white snow to the sound of silence. To this day, when I want to think about the stillness within, I am transported to this place and space of absolute, sheer silence and the ability to fully breathe life in and feel the pulse of the earth beneath the layers of rich snow.

Here, a mysterious and mystical cave temple was discovered, referred to as *The Temple of Destiny* or *Temple of the Chosen One*. Here within the cave monastery, you could see carved images on the walls of *The Star of David* and a Chinese *Yin Yang* symbol that you could see from the single source of light that enters the cave from a hole in the ceiling. The caretaker (a man with blue eyes like I'd never seen before, the whitest of hair and pale skin and who did not speak English) permitted us to enter the cave, which does not get a lot of visitors, let alone tourists. Our tour guide was our interpreter, and he told us that, for whatever reason, the caretaker welcomed *me* to step beyond the cordoned-off barrier to the altar. I charged my clear quartz generator crystal to amplify this extraordinary place's unique and mystical energies. This crystal has been charged and amplified by Mother Earth all over the globe as I embraced Mother Gaia inside of me, our ancestral mother who is said to have given birth to all the elements of the world.

May you find deep connection through your ongoing daily rituals and the power of Mother Gaia.

Affirmation

"Every day, I grow and glow as I embrace my inner Goddess awareness, and I courageously shine my light into the world."

Seed #13

When you honour, cherish and send loving energy toward your home, you permit yourself to do the same within. The external environment aligns with the internal environment, and harmony and respect prevail.

By bringing the sacred into your home and the rituals you create throughout your day, you enable further nourishment to your womb and the ability to water the seeds of your glorious future.

Afterword

An Australian summer can herald some of the hottest weather on the planet with its scorching, unrelenting heat. However, winter can be just as unforgiving at times with its bitterly cold breezes and frosty air.

Some years ago, while completing further studies, I immersed myself in the beauty of the terrain of the Blue Mountains, a couple of hours' drive west of Sydney, Australia. The Blue Mountains exhibit an abundance of wildlife. One frosty winter morning, I was out for my morning walk, complete with a beanie, gloves and thermals before class commenced. The days may have been crisp and cool; however, the upside was that the sky above was clear and blue, and the stars that twinkled in the night sky were always mesmerising.

On this particular crisp morning, I could hear the various calls of a specific bird nearby. I looked around to see what it was, and it was a lyrebird who was foraging around in the bushes.

I had long learned to slow down and listen to the call of nature, and so I heard this wise bird's message for me. Intently, I tuned into the world around me and tuned even deeper into the world within. The message I received from the Australian lyrebird was loud and clear:

> "Listen to the song in your heart, and let that be the voice of your soul that the world hears."

Later that day, I looked further into the symbology of the lyrebird, and I made some fantastic discoveries regarding the lyrebird:

1. It reminds us to create our own unique song;
2. It allows us to face our fears and find our authentic voice;
3. It acts as a link to ancient and ancestral voices by channelling spirit;
4. It allows us to find sacred places to practice connection to hear our messages. A lyrebird's habitat is often secretive and hidden, so it needs to go within to find that place to reflect and gather;
5. It keeps its sacred space clean and de-clutters to create a clear space for spirit. Lyrebirds are elegant and tidy, scraping leaf litter and dirt to create a beautiful space within the forest. The same can be said for attracting energy and creativity in our lives. The de-cluttering and scraping away can be physical, mental, emotional or spiritual. It's essentially about getting clarity in our lives. Letting go of what no longer serves us and weighs us down;
6. It acts as a teacher to help others find their voice and sing;
7. It has an Aboriginal dreamtime story associated with it that suggests that it's through singing our own song that we help others come to life alongside us.

I found that the symbology of the lyrebird so easily relates to aspects of us as women connecting to our voice, our heart and womb and allowing access to the gateway of the Goddess within.

There has been a yearning inside of me to be seen and heard. That yearning and longing to reclaim the inner Goddess is one that I feel so many women like yourself have also been leaning into, particularly in our current times and state of global consciousness. I now understand that a part of this longing has been to bring out the Goddess from inside me. Then in turn, help other women like yourself to do the same, allowing the inner Goddess to play her role in the world around us. Hearing the Goddess's call stirs ancient remembering; however, choosing to answer her call is when we really commence stepping into our divine feminine power.

It is not something outside of ourselves that we seek on the journey to awakening the inner Goddess. The Goddess within every woman has been held within all her life. She has been patiently waiting for you to step into the fullness of the woman that has always existed since the beginning of time.

Living the way of the Goddess does not happen solely on a weekend retreat or by becoming a student of ancient philosophy. Living the way of the Goddess happens daily, moment by moment. It happens with how you view your world, interact within it, connect to others on your life's journey, and the lessons learned along the way. To embrace the fullness of what life has to offer, a part of this includes reclaiming your femininity.

The 13 seeds presented to you in this book outline ways to help reclaim your inner Goddess toward wholehearted living, not just sometimes, but always. I soulfully and purposefully selected 13 chapters for the significance that the number 13 has, being the Goddess number connecting you to the divine feminine and the 13 lunar cycles within a year.

You may now choose to weave these 13 seeds into your daily living for your most empowered potential as a woman.

The 13 seeds in review:
1. The ability to access the wisdom from within your essence as a woman to see that any wound can be transformed into pearls of wisdom;

2. To harness the use of the rhythm of the physical body you have been gifted in this life to honour the cycles of your menstrual wisdom, which extends beyond into menopause;
3. Allowing yourself to be in alignment with the rhythm and cycle of Grandmother Moon and the gifts she brings us at each moon phase;
4. Welcoming and receiving the gift of menopause when the time comes with wide open arms while also acknowledging that this special rite of passage is one to be revered;
5. Bringing forward the ways of the ancients into modern times, especially at your personal moon time to acknowledge the need for rest as a crucial part of a woman's world;
6. Remembering where you came from, your ancient, ancestral roots and how these connections have helped to shape the courageous woman you are today;
7. The ability to use the art of meditation and your connection to the earth's energies to ignite further the flame that has always been inside of you by listening to your inner voice;
8. Acknowledging the lessons learned throughout your time as a maiden, mother and crone (remembering that these phases are cyclic throughout our life) and accessing this wisdom for future personal growth;
9. Bringing forgiveness into your life as a major healing catalyst for change, setting you free from the chains that bind;
10. Connection to your spirit guides regularly and allowing them to become your sacred allies;

11. Daily connection to the natural world around you and the elements to keep you grounded, centred and intuitively empowered;
12. Gathering the support of like-minded sisters to help elevate you on your path;
13. Acknowledging the archetypes within to witness all of your personality traits and embrace the wise woman who has always been within.

The final aspect to remember along your path toward tomorrow, is to understand that your strength, courage and power to be all you can be is through your sacred chalice, which is that of your womb.

Like the wise women of the Amazon Jungle, allow yourself to remember that *the womb is not a place to store fear and pain; the womb is to create and to give birth to life* (be it a child, a vision, a dream, or a project).

There isn't another woman on the planet who was born to be you; this is your unique life and purpose and your time to emerge out of the shadows and embrace your light fully.

It's time to rise and unlock the woman you were born to be. She who has been waiting is now set free to be all she ever dreamed possible and much more.

This book has enabled me as a woman to receive the cathartic healing I needed, to further embrace my inner Goddess and the path toward fulfilling my most empowered potential. We magnetise a life we love through healing our wounds, receiving our lessons and cherishing all parts of ourselves. Thank you for your part in joining me on this exciting adventure and helping to weave the tapestry of threads that connect us to each other through global consciousness.

It is my heartfelt wish that along your adventures within the wisdom of your womanly essence, this book has helped to further ignite the Goddess within you. May you continue your journey with the inner strength and courage to know that you have always been more than enough.

From my heart and womb to yours, you have my love now and forever more.

Kerry

xx

> *"Listen to the song in your heart, and let that be the voice of your soul that the world hears."*

Acknowledgements

Writing this book has been one of the most outstanding achievements of my life. I could not have written it without the unwavering and loving support of my ever-loyal husband, Gianni and my wise daughter, Cara. They have both been instrumental in shaping the woman I am today, and I am forever grateful for their love and strength in my life.

To my cherished mother Jill, words cannot express my love for you and the bond we share from generation to generation. Thank you for birthing me into this world. Alongside my dad John, I cannot think of any parents I would rather have to call my own and share my life with.

My gratitude pours abundantly toward Denise Linn, Meadow Linn, LuAnn Cibik, Kyla Tustin and the extended Linn Academy for supporting my dreams and helping me to embrace my inner potential.

To my beautiful friends, extended family and the many clients who have come into my life over the years; thank you for all I have learned and for allowing me to grow.

Lastly, to *you* as my reader, thank you from the bottom of my heart for enabling me to reach a lifelong dream of becoming an author. We each have stories to tell, and we each have something to impart to the world. I hope this book has enriched your life in some way.

May we all see and know our worth and acknowledge how one creative spark ignites another toward a life above and beyond our wildest dreams.

Resources

The work you have undertaken and started to delve into within this book is a journey for life. You may come back time and time again to keep working with the exercises and discovering more about yourself in the healing process.

Each day we have the opportunity to make our life even brighter than the previous one. However, as we move through our emotions and witness our inner wounds there can be some triggers for you along the road. Take your time, it is not a race and be gentle with yourself as you continue your adventures of womanhood.

If you wish to dive even deeper, feel welcome to join me at www.kerrydalzotto.com and I would be honoured to assist you further on your path toward healing and accessing your full power and potential.

www.ingramcontent.com/pod-product-compliance
Lightning Source LLC
Chambersburg PA
CBHW040740020526
44107CB00084B/2813